T0155537

Angular for Business

Awaken the Advocate Within and Become the Angular Expert at Work

Michael D. Callaghan

Apress®

Angular for Business: Awaken the Advocate Within and Become the Angular Expert at Work

Michael D. Callaghan
Celebration, FL, USA

ISBN-13 (pbk): 978-1-4842-9608-0   ISBN-13 (electronic): 978-1-4842-9609-7
https://doi.org/10.1007/978-1-4842-9609-7

Managing Director, Apress Media LLC: Welmoed Spahr
Acquisitions Editor: James Robinson-Prior
Development Editor: James Markham
Coordinating Editor: Shaul Elson

Cover image by Image by xiSerge from Pixabay

Distributed to the book trade worldwide by Apress Media, LLC, 1 New York Plaza, New York, NY 10004, U.S.A. Phone 1-800-SPRINGER, fax (201) 348-4505, e-mail orders-ny@springer-sbm.com, or visit www.springeronline.com. Apress Media, LLC is a California LLC and the sole member (owner) is Springer Science + Business Media Finance Inc (SSBM Finance Inc). SSBM Finance Inc is a **Delaware** corporation.

For information on translations, please e-mail booktranslations@springernature.com; for reprint, paperback, or audio rights, please e-mail bookpermissions@springernature.com.

Apress titles may be purchased in bulk for academic, corporate, or promotional use. eBook versions and licenses are also available for most titles. For more information, reference our Print and eBook Bulk Sales web page at http://www.apress.com/bulk-sales.

Any source code or other supplementary material referenced by the author in this book is available to readers on GitHub (https://github.com/Apress). For more detailed information, please visit https://www.apress.com/gp/services/source-code.

Paper in this product is recyclable

Table of Contents

About the Author

Michael D. Callaghan is a highly experienced software developer with over 25 years of professional experience in the field. Throughout his career, he has developed a reputation as an expert in delivering high-quality software solutions for a wide range of clients and industries.

Michael began learning to program computers in 1981 during high school when the data processing teacher took pity on a young ninth grader and let him borrow time on the county's HP 2000 to teach himself BASIC. This sparked a passion for software development that has never waned. Though his early career took a ten-year detour, Michael finally began writing software professionally in 1995 and has been doing so ever since.

In addition to his technical skills, Michael has a deep understanding of the challenges and pitfalls of working in the tech industry. He has written several books on the impact of poor communication on software development projects, which are available on Amazon and have become widely recognized as essential reading for anyone working in the field. His insights and advice have helped many organizations avoid costly mistakes and improve the overall quality of their communications.

Overall, Michael is a well-respected and experienced professional in the field of software development, with a passion for sharing his knowledge and experience with others.

About the Technical Reviewer

Vadim Atamanenko is an experienced software engineer with over 25 years of experience, a member of the IEEE Association, and an active participant in the scientific community. He is the author of numerous scientific articles, an expert in international hackathons, and a lecturer in software development courses and currently serves as the Head of the Development Department at Freedom Life Insurance Company. Vadim also shares his knowledge and expertise through more than 40 articles published in online publications in two languages (English and Russian). He is always open to meeting new people and exchanging knowledge.

You can contact him and learn more about his work on his LinkedIn profile: www.linkedin.com/in/vadim-atamanenko/.

Introduction

In late spring 2018, my manager presented me with intriguing news. Our executive director had noticed that while Angular was widely used across his organization, the in-house developers lacked extensive experience with it.

They pondered various methods to address this gap, ranging from subscribing to video courses, purchasing books, to hiring an external training firm to conduct the required training.

My manager then suggested, "What if we ask Mike Callaghan to handle it?" Thus, in an executive meeting, he proposed that I be the one to train our software developers on Angular.

My Angular Journey

My engagement with Angular dates back to AngularJS 1.2. My debut Angular application was a mobile swimming coach, crafted with the Ionic Framework and AngularJS.

Presently, I almost exclusively create web applications using Angular. Though I confess, I have briefly experimented with React – even going as far as writing a book on using React with Ionic.

Whenever I embark on a new application, whether for personal or professional use, I usually begin with Angular.

What's in This Book?

This book is a compilation of essays that I've written for diverse technical audiences over the past year or so. These pieces directly or indirectly pertain to Angular development.

However, this book is not intended for beginners in web development – there are ample resources catering to that audience. Instead, this book is aimed at seasoned web developers who have some experience or familiarity with Angular.

The content, admittedly, bears my biases, much like the broader Angular ecosystem.

I illustrate solutions that have proven effective for me and my team. Other approaches and solutions may also yield results, but I won't focus on them here.

The contents of this book reflect my experience, and I hope they offer valuable insights for your learning journey.

PART I

Core Concepts

CHAPTER 1

A Quick Introduction to TypeScript

You will probably need to introduce coworkers to TypeScript. Here's how you can do that.

At my day job, I was asked by my leadership to provide an introduction to TypeScript, Angular, and Node to a group of experienced software developers. Many of these folks are "senior" or higher, a few with more years of experience than I have. Despite their combined 200+ years of development, they have not used these technologies. This chapter is what I showed them: An introduction to TypeScript for experienced developers.

TypeScript Playground

To help internalize the concepts you are about to see, consider opening a browser to `www.typescriptlang.org/play/`. This website lets you enter TypeScript in one text area and see the corresponding JavaScript instantly. It also provides helpful feedback in the case of TypeScript errors. I find it very handy to understand what's going on during the TypeScript transpilation process.

Types!

The first thing to understand about TypeScript is that – surprise – it has types. It supports the basic types you would expect, such as strings and numbers. You can supply the type explicitly, as in the top examples. Or you may omit the type and supply a value instead. If you provide a variable with a value, then TypeScript will infer the type automatically.

```
// Explicit Type Declaration
let isDone: boolean = false;
let decimal: number = 6;
let hex: number = 0xf00d;
let binary: number = 0b1010;
let octal: number = 0o744;
```

```
// Implicit Type Declaration
let isDone = false;
let decimal = 6;
let hex = 0xf00d;
let binary = 0b1010;
let octal = 0o744;
```

Don't be fooled, however. Type inference still means the variable has a type; you simply did not need to set it. Trying to assign a number to a string will still be an error.

Strings

TypeScript includes support for strings. You can use either single or double quotes for string constants, but you should be consistent. Many teams prefer one or the other and use tools to enforce that preference.

A third type of quote, the backtick, is used to create templated strings. The sentence variable in the following code is a three-line string – yes, a templated string can include line breaks. The expression inside the ${ } is evaluated and that value replaces the entire ${ } construct.

```
let color: string = 'red';
let fullName = "Bob Bobbington";
let age = 37;
let sentence = `Hello, my name is ${ fullName }.

I'll be ${ age + 1 } years old next month.`;

console.log(sentence);

// Output:
"Hello, my name is Bob Bobbington.

I'll be 38 years old next month."
```

It is interesting to see how a template string is represented in modern JavaScript: it's the same thing! With older versions of JavaScript it would have been converted into an old-fashioned string assignment with the expected concatenations.

Arrays

TypeScript supports arrays. Here we are creating a list as an array of numbers, as indicated by the square brackets following the type. This was not necessary, of course, as the value on the right side of the equal sign clearly indicates that it is an array of numbers. Most of the time, you only want to set the type explicitly if you are not also providing a value at the same time.

```
let list: number[] = [1, 2, 3];
let list = [1, 2, 3];
```

Enums

Enumerations, or Enums, allow you to provide a set of human-readable values, which represent the only legal values a variable can contain. In this case, I have defined an enum named Color, which contains three values: Red, Green, and Blue. A constant or variable of this type is only allowed to take on one of those three values. As you can see, to use the value on the right side of an assignment, you need to specify the Enum name, followed by a dot and then the enum value. Attempting to set a non-existent value is an error.

```
enum Color {
  Red,
  Green,
  Blue,
}
const green: Color = Color.Green;

const purple = Color.Purple; // Error!
```

String Literal Types

String literal types in TypeScript allow you to specify a type that can only have a certain set of specified string values. This provides a way to define a type that can only be one of a few different strings. It's akin to an enum, but for strings. The syntax is simple: you define a type to be equal to one or more string literals, separated by the pipe character (|).

This construct proves beneficial in situations where you want to ensure that a variable or a function parameter only accepts certain specific string values. This results in safer code by catching potential errors at compile time. You can think of these as creating a sort of enumerated type for strings, ensuring the value is one from a specified list.

Consider this example where we have a type Fruit that could either be ''Apple'', ''Banana'', or ''Cherry''. Trying to assign any other string value to a variable of type Fruit would result in a TypeScript error.

```
type Fruit = "Apple" | "Banana" | "Cherry";

let myFruit: Fruit;

myFruit = "Apple"; // This is valid
myFruit = "Banana"; // This is also valid
myFruit = "Pear"; // Error! 'Pear' is not assignable to
type 'Fruit'
```

Similarly, we can use string literal types to restrict the parameters that a function accepts:

```
type Direction = "Up" | "Down" | "Left" | "Right";

function move(direction: Direction) {
  // function body
}

move("Up"); // This is valid
move("Down"); // This is also valid
move("North"); // Error! Argument of type '"North"' is not
assignable to parameter of type 'Direction'
```

In this case, the move function only accepts ''Up'', ''Down'', ''Left'', or ''Right'' as valid directions. Attempting to call move(''North'') would result in a TypeScript error, as "North" is not a valid Direction. This aids in creating more robust, error-resistant code by ensuring only expected values are passed.

String literal types share some similarities with enums in that they both limit the possible values a variable can have to a predefined set. However, there are some key differences. With enums, the values are numerical (unless you manually assign string values to the enum members), whereas with string literal types, the values are, of course, strings. This difference becomes significant in contexts where the actual value matters, such as when the value is used in comparisons or displayed to the user.

In Angular templates, for example, string literal types can be more convenient than enums. This is because Angular templates are essentially chunks of HTML, which is a text-based format. When you bind a property in an Angular template to an enum value, the underlying numerical value is used, which often isn't what you want. On the other hand, when you bind to a string literal type, the string value is used, which is typically more useful in a text-based context like HTML.

For instance, consider a scenario where we have a component that displays a status message. If we use an enum to represent the status, we would need to create a mapping from the enum values to the corresponding status messages. But with a string literal type, we can directly use the status values in the template, which makes the code more straightforward and easier to understand.

Here is an example:

```
type Status = "Loading" | "Success" | "Error";

@Component({
  selector: "my-app",
  template: `<div>{{ status }}</div>`,
})
export class AppComponent {
  status: Status = "Loading";
}
```

In this case, the status property is a string literal type that could be "Loading," "Success," or "Error." The value of the status property is directly usable in the template, which simplifies the code compared to using an enum.

Interfaces

Interfaces are supported as a pure TypeScript construct, and do not compile to any sort of JavaScript whatsoever. Go ahead and enter an interface definition into the TypeScript playground. Don't let that fool you into thinking that they aren't useful.

An interface can be used to enforce the shape of data being passed into a function, or to help when initializing a strongly typed object from an object literal. The interface defined here consists of four string values and requires that any object defined as a Member contain an email address, a first name, and a last name. The phone number is optional, denoted by the question mark at the end of the field name.

Using interfaces for data objects will help the TypeScript compiler help you prevent common typos when initializing objects, without resorting to building complete classes where they aren't strictly necessary.

```
interface Member {
  email: string;
  firstName: string;
  lastName: string;
  phone?: string; // The ? indicates this is optional
}
```

Object and Array Literals

For example, imagine we want to initialize an array of Member objects. Specifying the type explicitly as Member[] will let the TypeScript compiler know to check that every object literal provided matches the Member interface definition. Notice that I am not providing a phone number, as that field was marked as optional in the interface.

```
const allMembers: Member[] = [
  { email: "1234@company.com", firstName: "Mike", lastName:
  "Smith" },
  { email: "2345@company.com", firstName: "Bob", lastName:
  "Johnson" },
  { email: "3456@company.com", firstName: "Debbie", lastName:
  "Jones" },
  { email: "4567@company.com", firstName: "Carol", lastName:
  "Brown" },
];
```

Had Member been defined as a class, we would need to use its constructor to define new Member objects, which would require more code, and end up a lot less readable than this method.

Classes in TypeScript

TypeScript also provides concrete classes. Here is a hypothetical class implementation of that same Member interface. As you can see, it is a lot more code, and in no way is it any more readable than simply using the interface.

```
class MemberImpl implements Member {
  email: string;
  firstName: string;
  lastName: string;
  phone?: string;

  constructor(email: string, firstName: string, lastName:
  string, phone: string = "") {
    this.email = email;
    this.firstName = firstName;
```

```
    this.lastName = lastName;
    this.phone = phone;
  }
}
```

My general recommendation is not to use a class unless and until you have code that needs to be added to it. I would argue even then that you think twice before adding code to a data object. Code such as validation should be done in a separate utility class. Leave your data objects clean, but that is a topic for another day.

Generics in TypeScript

Like many other modern languages, TypeScript supports Generics. This allows you to create common code that operates the same, regardless of the type passed to it. Illustrated here, we show a potential interface representing a stack of objects, consisting of three functions: pop, push, and length.

```
interface Stack<T> {
  pop(): T;
  push(item: T);
  length(): number;
}
```

Notice the angle brackets containing a single T in the interface definition. This declares the interface as being a generic, with T representing the compile-time type. Using the T is a common convention, but it can be any unused identifier. The function pop() returns a single object of that type; push() accepts an item parameter of the same type. The length() function returns a single number.

In the following, you can see the creation of two variables of type Stack, each passing a different type. As you may guess, you cannot pass a parameter of the wrong type to any of its functions.

```
let numbers: Stack<number>;
let names: Stack<string>;
names.push("Mike"); // OK
names.push(5); // Error
```

Arrow Functions in TypeScript

TypeScript supports arrow functions, which can be used in place of the anonymous functions you may be used to. In the examples shown here, we are calling the window's setTimeout function to delay for five seconds, and then show an alert.

```
window.setTimeout(function () {
  alert("It has been five seconds!");
}, 5000);

window.setTimeout(() => {
  alert("It has been five seconds!");
}, 5000);

window.ondblclick = (ev: MouseEvent) => {
  // `this` refers to the class
  this.mouseX = ev.clientX;
  this.mouseY = ev.clientY;
};
```

At first glance, you are probably wondering what the big deal is. We removed the keyword function and added an equal sign and a greater-than sign (that is the arrow). This yields a grand total savings of three characters, so why bother, right?

In my mind, the most important aspect of arrow functions is the fact that the anonymous function to the right of the arrow does NOT redefine the this variable. If you've ever been bitten by JavaScript redefining this inside your functions, you will appreciate that behavior. Now you can write event handlers inside of a class, and still refer to class variables properly, simply by referring to them with the this object inside your event handler arrow function.

Promises in TypeScript

TypeScript supports promises, so you do not need to rely on an external library such as Bluebird.

A Promise is a guarantee that a function will complete at some unknown time in the future. The classic example of this is an HTTP call. When you make an HTTP request, you are waiting for the remote server to return data to you. If you wait for that reply, your code is stuck and cannot do anything else, including responding to user interaction. Because of that, many asynchronous functions return a promise instead of the actual result. When the function finally does complete, the promise is said to "resolve." If there is an error, the promise is said to "reject." The way you handle that in code is straightforward, but odd if you haven't seen it before.

```
function getMyIpAddress(): Promise<string> {
  return fetch("https://api.ipify.org/?format=json")
    .then((response) => response.json())
    .catch((error) => console.log(error));
}

getMyIpAddress()
  .then((ip) => console.log(`Your IP address is: ${JSON.
  stringify(ip)}`))
  .catch((error) => console.log(error));
```

Here we see a simple implementation of a function to retrieve the public facing IP address of the browser in which it is running. Notice we are combining multiple concepts here. The function returns a promise of type `string`. The calling function calls `fetch`, which also returns a promise. However, it also calls two more functions on that returned promise. The `then` function accepts a function to be called when the promise itself has resolved. In this example, I am passing an arrow function that converts the response to `json` and returns that value. I am using a shortcut here in that if an arrow function only returns the results of a single expression, you can omit both the `return` keyword and the semi-colon.

Inside the `then` function, I'm simply logging the response object, which I have named `ip` in this case. You can do that with arrow functions. The signature only specifies the number (and sometimes the types) of the parameters, but you can name them anything you want. Notice also that I'm calling `JSON.stringify(ip)` to convert the `ip` object into text that can be read. Otherwise, the output would be simply be `[object object]`, which doesn't help anyone.

The `then` function itself returns a promise, which I use to call its `catch` function. `catch` also accepts a function to be called in case of an error. Here I am providing another arrow function, which accepts the error object and logs it.

Essentially, what is happening here is that the URL provided is requested. At some point in the future, one of two things will happen:

- Either the HTTP call succeeds, at which point it is "resolved," and then function passed to `then()` is called.

- Or the HTTP call fails, the promise is "rejected," and the function passed to `catch()` is called.

Finally, notice also that the getMyIpAddress() function itself returns a promise, so calling it will look very similar. This is a common pattern you will see repeated often in TypeScript.

Promises: async/await

An alternative pattern to working with promises is to use async and await. Any function marked with the keyword async can call await on a promise, allowing the code to appear more imperative and hopefully a little easier to read.

In this example, I have rewritten getMyIpAddress() and its client with async and await. No more .then() or .catch(). Instead, the functionality looks and reads exactly like a function without any asynchronous calls. However, this is purely an illusion, as you can see if you paste that code into the TypeScript Playground.

```
async function getMyIpAddress(): Promise<string> {
  const response = await fetch("https://api.ipify.
  org/?format=json");
  const data = await response.json();
  return data.ip;
}

async function run(): Promise<void> {
  try {
    const ip = await getMyIpAddress();
    console.log(`Your IP address is: ${ip}`);
  } catch (error) {
    console.log(error);
  }
}

run();
```

As I said previously, every function that has an `await` keyword must be marked as `async`. This is because the `await` keyword can only be used inside an `async` function. In this code, since the `getMyIpAddress` function contains an `await` statement, it needs to be declared as `async`.

To ensure the code runs smoothly, I wrapped the execution inside another function called `run`. This function serves as the entry point for executing the code. By marking it as `async`, we can use the `await` keyword inside `run` to pause the execution and wait for the asynchronous operations to complete, such as the `getMyIpAddress` function.

When `run` is called, it triggers the execution of the code inside it. The `await getMyIpAddress()` line within `run` causes the function to pause and wait for the `getMyIpAddress` function to resolve and return the IP address. Once the IP address is obtained, it is stored in the `ip` variable, and the code proceeds to the next line, which logs the IP address to the console.

By wrapping the execution inside the `run` function and marking it as `async`, we ensure that the `await` keyword can be used within the function, allowing us to handle the asynchronous operations gracefully.

When the `fetch` function is called with the `await` keyword, the `getMyIpAddress` function exits immediately.

When `fetch` resolves successfully, the result of the promise is set as the value of the `response` constant, and then execution continues with the next line of code. If the promise rejects, the error will be thrown as an exception, which is caught higher up.

Likewise, the call to `getMyIpAddress` works the same way. Execution is halted at that line (but the application keeps running as normal). When the promise returned by `getMyIpAddress` resolves, its response is set as the value of the constant `ip`, and execution picks up from that point. Any exceptions thrown will be caught in the `catch` block.

Using `async` and `await` is wonderful in that your code looks more traditional, but you should never forget there are promises underneath the magic.

Some Are More Equal Than Others

When are values equal? The answer may surprise you. While not specific to TypeScript, this topic has bitten many new JavaScript and TypeScript developers. Consider the following example.

```
console.log("1" == 1); // true
console.log("" == 0); // true
console.log("1" == [1]); // true
```

If you expected those all to be false, then this explanation is for you. If you are following along in the TypeScript playground, you will notice that it warns you not to do those things.

The problem is that JavaScript will coerce from one type to another to make the comparison, even if that is not what you want or expect. The solution is to use === instead of ==, which says not to use coercion. Thus, each of the following lines return the expected value of false.

```
console.log("1" === 1); // false
console.log("" === 0); // false
console.log("1" === [1]); // false
```

It is recommended that you use === for comparisons, and most teams will use a tool to ensure it.

What About var?

You may have noticed that I did not use the var keyword in any of my examples. TypeScript, along with more recent versions of JavaScript, introduces two new ways of declaring variables (and constants), respectively, let and const.

17

The important difference to note is that objects declared with var are "function-scoped," while those declared with let are "block scoped." Consider this example.

```
for (var i = 0; i < 100; i++) {
  if (i % 3 === 0) {
    console.log("FIZZ");
  }
  if (i % 5 === 0) {
    console.log("BUZZ");
  }
  if (i % 5 && i % 3) {
    console.log(i);
  }
}

console.log(i); // 100
```

In this case, you might expect i not be legal on that last line, given that it was defined as part of the for loop. But because var is function-scoped, it is defined anywhere in the function in which it appears, even if it were declared really deeply.

Had we used let instead of var, the generated JavaScript will be identical, but the TypeScript compiler will flag the use of i in console.log to be an error. The recommendation is to use let instead of var in your TypeScript code.

The other new keyword, const, works exactly like let, in that the object defined will be block-scoped. However, with const you must provide a value. Further, once declared, its value can never be changed.

```
const myName = "Mike";
myName = "Bob"; // Error - cannot redefine
```

This rule applies only to the named object, and not any of its members (in the case of a complex object or array). For example, you can manipulate the members of an array. You can also add, change, or remove properties to an object. You simply cannot reassign its value.

```
const mike: Member = { email: "1234@company.com", firstName:
"Mike", lastName: "Smith" };
mike.email = "mike";

// These are fine
const allMembers: Member[] = [];
allMembers.push(mike);

// Errors - may not redefine constants
allMembers = [];
mike = { email: "2345@company.com", firstName: "Bob", lastName:
"Johnson" };
```

Summary

As we've explored in this chapter, TypeScript offers a rich and robust set of features that enhance the JavaScript development experience, ensuring type safety and facilitating more reliable, maintainable code. From simple Types, Arrays, Enums, Interfaces, classes, to String Literal Types, TypeScript provides us with the tools to write clear, self-documenting code, where entities and their expected behaviors are clearly defined.

Digging Deeper into TypeScript

We've only just scratched the surface of what TypeScript can do. With its other features like Generics, Decorators, and advanced type manipulation capabilities such as Mapped Types and Conditional Types, TypeScript has the power to revolutionize how you write JavaScript code.

Moreover, TypeScript's compatibility with JavaScript means that you can start benefiting from it at your own pace. You can start by annotating existing JavaScript code, gradually adopting TypeScript's features as you become more comfortable with them, or even start a new project fully in TypeScript.

The true power of TypeScript comes not just from its features, but from the way it fosters better coding practices, encouraging clarity, precision, and predictability, which in turn leads to more robust and maintainable software.

Learning and Mastering TypeScript

Remember, the learning journey doesn't stop here. If you want to delve deeper and truly master TypeScript, a wealth of information and resources awaits you. The official TypeScript website, `www.typescriptlang.org`, is a great starting point. It provides detailed documentation, examples, and guides that can help you understand the nuances of TypeScript and apply it effectively in your projects.

Conclusion

In the end, TypeScript is a powerful ally in the world of JavaScript development. Embracing TypeScript is embracing a future of robust, scalable, and error-resistant code. The journey into TypeScript might be new and challenging, but the rewards are worth the effort. So, keep exploring, keep learning, and most importantly, enjoy the journey into TypeScript.

CHAPTER 2

A Gentle Introduction to Angular

The aim of this chapter is to offer a gentle introduction to Angular, providing your team with the foundational knowledge required to navigate the platform effectively. This is not an exhaustive guide to mastering Angular, but rather an initiation into its unique idioms and patterns – those peculiar "Angularisms" that form the essence of its syntax and structure.

We'll journey through the fundamental elements of Angular, presenting the core concepts in a clear and accessible manner. This will enable your team members to confidently dive into the code, equipped with an understanding of Angular's fundamental principles. This initial understanding is crucial, as it will serve as the foundation upon which they will continue to build their knowledge and expertise.

To work through the example in this chapter, open a browser to Stackblitz. This will provide you with an immediate sandbox where you can follow along. As soon as you do, you should see the following code in the center panel, a file called main.ts.

Raw URL: `https://stackblitz.com/fork/angular`

```
import 'zone.js/dist/zone';
import { Component } from '@angular/core';
import { CommonModule } from '@angular/common';
import { bootstrapApplication } from '@angular/platform-browser';
```

```
@Component({
  selector: 'my-app',
  standalone: true,
  imports: [CommonModule],
  template: `
    <h1>Hello from {{ name }}!</h1>
    <a target="_blank" href="https://angular.io/start">
      Learn more about Angular
    </a>
  `,
})
export class App {
  name = 'Angular';
}

bootstrapApplication(App);
```

Angular's Concept of Separation of Concerns

Let us start by talking about Angular's concept of separation of concerns. In this sample app, you probably don't see much separation, but it's there. As you create larger apps, you certainly would.

Personally, I would not recommend you combine all these together in one file, except in the simplest of components. That said, there are many proponents of keeping all your component code in one file. Find your own balance; it is probably somewhere in between "always" and "never" doing this.

Understanding Components

In Angular, UI functionality is encapsulated in components. A component can represent anything from a piece of text, a button, a form, or even an entire page. Components can contain other components, and they can communicate with each other through well-defined interfaces.

You specify that a TypeScript class is a component using the @Component decorator. Decorators provide additional information by annotating or modifying classes or class members.

In this case, the component decorator provides additional metadata to Angular about how the class will behave.

Understanding Attributes

The `selector` attribute tells Angular to expose this component using the HTML tag `<my-app>`.

The `standalone` attribute tells Angular that this component does not reside in a separate NgModule. Standalone components were first introduced as a developer preview in Angular 15.2.

The `imports` attribute indicates that the code in this component makes use of functionality found inside "CommonModule." We will use some of these functionality later in this chapter, so it's important that we import it.

The `template` attribute directly contains the HTML markup.

Understanding the Component Class

The executable portion of the component code is found inside the class definition. This one contains a single line of code, meaning it is not doing much.

Even though everything is inside one file, this is what I mean by a "separation of concerns." The code, markup, and styles are all separated from one another.

Understanding the Markup

Take a look at the markup. It is a TypeScript templated string literal containing pure HTML content.

```
<h1>Hello from {{name}}!</h1>
<a target="_blank" href="https://angular.io/start">
  Learn more about Angular
</a>
```

Notice the first line contains a common HTML tag, <h1>.

Inside of that tag is an attribute called name, set to the value {{ name }}. This is an Angular "one-way" binding expression. During the page rendering phase, Angular sees that expression, and knows to set the value of the name attribute to the run-time value of the variable name on the component. It would probably be less confusing if they used a different variable name.

Now, change the name variable inside the component code and give it a different value. I changed mine to look like this.

```
export class App {
  name = 'Mike';
}
```

Look at Figure 2-1, the result that appears in the right-hand pane. The value you provided should be displayed instead of the original value.

Hello from Mike!

Learn more about Angular

Figure 2-1. *The output of the program, which says "Hello from Mike!"*

Hello Component

Let's create a simple component we can use to encapsulate the previous message, so that we can reuse it later. In the left panel, find the src folder and right-click it. A menu will appear offering a number of options. Select the one labeled "Angular Generator" and then select Component, as shown in Figure 2-2.

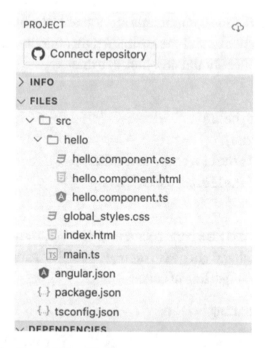

Figure 2-2. *The Stackblitz file layout*

Name your new component Hello. Stackblitz will create a new folder named hello containing three files.

Here, you will be able to see a true separation of concerns, though I would have been fine with keeping it all together for what will be a trivial example. Again, you will eventually find your own balance. There is no right or wrong.

Open up the file `hello.component.ts` and look at its implementation. The first thing you may notice is that its markup is defined in a different file. It also has a `styleUrls` array that we didn't see before. This is the more traditional way to define an Angular component, clearly separating its imperative component code from its declarative markup and styles. The component itself is pretty bland, containing no code at all yet.

It's also missing something critical, at least for our purposes here. This new component is neither marked as standalone, nor is it part of a larger `NgModule`. As standalone components are arguably the future of Angular, let's fix it by adding a `standalone` attribute right after the `selector`. Your `@Component` decorator should now look like this:

```
@Component({
  selector: 'app-hello',
  standalone: true,
  templateUrl: './hello.component.html',
  styleUrls: ['./hello.component.css']
})
```

The component class's constructor and ngOnInit function are both blank. You can go ahead and leave them. It won't hurt anything. Above the constructor, add a single line of code:

```
@Input() name: string = '';
```

@Input is another decorator, which specifies that name is a string attribute that can be provided in the markup of any client that uses this component. Let's do that now.

If you see that @Input is underlined in red, it means that StackBlitz didn't import it for you. See Figure 2-3. If you click on @Input and look carefully at the beginning of the line, you should see a little lightbulb icon. Click it and StackBlitz will usually offer to do the right thing for you. In this case, its default option is to add the import for us.

```
port class HelloComponent implements OnInit {
  @Input() name: string = '';

  ┌──────────────────────────────────────────┐
  │ Update import from "@angular/core"        │
  └──────────────────────────────────────────┘
    Change spelling to 'oninput'

}
```

Figure 2-3. *Screenshot showing the automatic import feature*

Alternatively, you can manually add it to the existing import line from '@angular/core', like this:

```
import {
  Component,
  Input,
  OnInit,
} from '@angular/core';
```

Either way, you should end up with a line like that one at the top of the file.

Now let's make this component do something interesting. Open the markup file, hello.component.html. Delete its contents and add a single line:

```
<h1>Hello from {{ name }}!</h1>
```

If this looks familiar, it's similar to what we already have seen in main.ts.

Component Reuse

The real power of creating a component like this is that you can reuse the component anywhere, simply replacing its name attribute, and it will render consistently.

Back in main.ts, we need to import the new component so that we can use it. Find the imports attribute. Notice its value is an array. Add HelloComponent to the array, right after CommonModule. It should now look like this:

```
imports: [CommonModule, HelloComponent],
```

If you did it correctly, StackBlitz automatically imported the HelloComponent at the top of the file and you'll see this line at the top of the file with the rest of the imports.

```
import { HelloComponent } from './hello/hello.component';
```

If that line isn't there, go ahead and click the lightbulb to add it automatically, or manually add it after the other import statements.

Import vs. Imports

The TypeScript import statement is used to import classes, functions, types, and other exported items from other TypeScript or JavaScript modules into the current file. These imports allow you to use external functionalities within your TypeScript code.

On the other hand, starting with Angular 15.2, the @Component decorator now includes an imports array. This array isn't related to TypeScript's import statement. Instead, it's specific to Angular and is used to provide the compilation context for standalone components. It includes all other components, directives, pipes, and NgModules that are used in the template of the standalone component.

So, while both involve the term "import", they serve different purposes.

Now that the HelloComponent is available to the component, replace the <h1> tag and its contents with a few copies of the <hello> tag and provide different names. Something like this, perhaps.

```
<app-hello name="{{ name }}"></app-hello>
<app-hello name="Greg"></app-hello>
<app-hello name="Jonathan"></app-hello>
<app-hello name="Neil"></app-hello>
```

Now the output should look something like that in Figure 2-4. Furthermore, we do not have to be concerned with how the <hello> tag works behind the scenes. We can simply reuse it.

Hello from Mike!

Hello from Greg!

Hello from Jonathan!

Hello from Neil!

Learn more about Angular

Figure 2-4. *Multiple Hello components with different names*

ngFor

But what if you have a bunch of names? Change the name variable on the component and make it an array called names.

```
names = ['Mike', 'Greg', 'Jonathan', 'Neil'];
```

The cool thing about reusing components this way is that you do not have to change the hello component at all. You simply need to change the calling code to use ngFor, an Angular directive used to create multiple instances of the hello component based on the number of elements in the referenced array.

You use an ngFor by providing it as an attribute to the element you want replicated. The value inside the quotes is the looping expression. It consists of the keyword *let* followed by the variable name to be used inside the element and any of its children, the keyword *of*, and the name of the array on the component to loop over.

Delete the individual app-hello tags, replacing them with a single tag with an ngFor expression, like this:

```
<app-hello
  *ngFor="let name of names"
  name="{{name}}"
/app-hello>
```

The asterisk, which is required, is an indication to Angular that this directive will manipulate the DOM, or the page's document object model, in some way.

One thing to be aware of when using this type of binding is that the expression inside the curly braces is always converted to a string. This can be an issue when you're trying to bind to an attribute that expects a boolean or a number.

Attribute Binding

There is another binding syntax that works with HTML attributes. If you want to set the value of an attribute to a value on your component, use square brackets around the attribute name. This is also a type of one-way data binding but instead of converting the value to a string, attribute binding will preserve the data type. For example, if we were binding a boolean in the TypeScript code, it will remain a boolean when passed to the HTML element attribute.

```
<app-hello
  *ngFor="let name of names"
  [name]="name"
/app-hello>
```

In general, if you're working with values that should maintain their type (like booleans or numbers), you should use property binding. If you're working with string values or you specifically need a string value, interpolation would be appropriate. I'll show you more about that soon.

HTML Event Binding

You can also bind to HTML events. Any event can become a trigger to execute a function on the component. The simplest way to illustrate that is to create a button and provide a click handler.

You do that by surrounding the event name (in this case, click) with parenthesis. Then inside the quotes, call the component function you want to execute.

You can pass parameters to the function, which is often the case when creating an event binding inside an *ngFor, passing the current looping variable to the event handler.

In this case, just call toggle(). Let's get rid of that <a> tag and replace it with the following code:

```
<button (click)="toggle()">Click Me</button>
```

Back inside the component class itself, we'll need to implement the toggle function. Add this code inside the app component, right after the names array.

```
isToggled = false;

toggle() {
  this.isToggled = !this.isToggled;
}
```

Now when you click the toggle button, the value of the isToggled variable will flip between true and false.

ngIf

The isToggled variable is useless until you do something with it. Add a new line inside the component's template. That's where ngIf comes in. It's used to conditionally add or remove an element from the DOM based on an expression. If the expression evaluates to a truthy value, the element is added to the DOM. If it's a falsy value, the element is removed. This makes ngIf very useful for controlling the visibility of elements based on conditions in your TypeScript code. Remember that, as a structural directive just like ngFor, ngIf is used with an asterisk (*) *before the directive in your templates, like this:* ngIf="condition".

In this case, let's add a paragraph tag, give it an ngIf directive, and set its condition to "isToggled." You should see output like Figure 2-5.

```
<p *ngIf="isToggled">I am toggled on!!!</p>
```

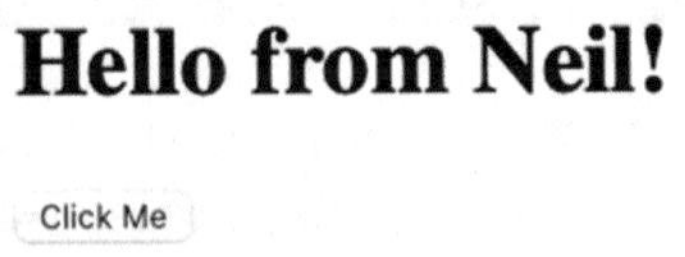

Hello from Neil!

Click Me

Figure 2-5. *Hello from Neil! but with the new paragraph missing*

Now as you click the button, that paragraph will appear and disappear, as in Figure 2-6.

Hello from Neil!

Click Me

I am toggled on!!!

Figure 2-6. *Hello from Neil! but with the new paragraph visible*

Those are the basics you need to know to work with Angular.

Summary

The concepts we've covered so far form the cornerstone of Angular development. They are the building blocks you need to get started with creating dynamic, robust Angular applications. However, Angular is a vast framework with numerous features and best practices. For more detailed and comprehensive information, the Angular official documentation is an invaluable resource. The raw URL is `https://angular.io`. It provides in-depth guidance on Angular's various features, from basics to advanced topics. And rest assured, this is just the beginning. Throughout the rest of this book, we'll delve deeper into Angular, exploring more complex concepts and features, building more intricate applications, and mastering this powerful framework.

CHAPTER 3

Angular CLI Quick Reference

One of the most powerful tools in the Angular ecosystem is the Angular Command Line Interface (CLI), also known as the ng CLI. The Angular CLI is an indispensable tool for Angular developers, providing a comprehensive set of commands that simplify and streamline the process of creating, scaffolding, and managing Angular applications. The CLI abstracts away much of the complexity and boilerplate code that comes with setting up a new Angular project, allowing you to focus on writing your application logic. The Angular CLI also supports a wide variety of custom tasks, reducing the need for manual configuration and setup in many project scenarios.

Installing NodeJS and NPM

The most straightforward way to install the Angular CLI is through npm, the Node Package Manager, which is the default package manager for Node.js. That means you'll need to install NodeJS and npm first. Most systems probably don't include them by default, so we'll assume you don't have them. If you do, feel free to skip this section.

© Michael D. Callaghan 2024
M. D. Callaghan, *Angular for Business*, https://doi.org/10.1007/978-1-4842-9609-7_3

For Windows and macOS

For Windows, macOS, and Linux, you can download Node.js and npm directly from the official Node.js website (`https://nodejs.org/`). The site provides pre-built installers for various platforms:

- Visit the Node.js downloads page here (`https://nodejs.org/en/download/`).

- Choose the appropriate installer for your platform (Windows or macOS).

- Download and run the installer, which will install both Node.js and npm on your system.

For Linux

- Most Linux distributions have Node.js available in their package repositories, which also includes npm. You can install Node.js and npm using your distribution's package manager. For example, on Ubuntu or Debian, you can use the following commands in your terminal:

  ```
  sudo apt update
  sudo apt install nodejs npm
  ```

- Alternatively, you can also download and run the Node.js installer from the Node.js website, similar to the process for Windows and macOS.

Alternative Node Version Manager

Node Version Manager (NVM) is a useful utility for managing multiple active Node.js versions. It allows you to install, uninstall, and switch between different versions of Node.js with ease. While NVM is a powerful tool, a detailed explanation of its use is beyond the scope of this book.

NVM exists for various platforms:

- For macOS and Linux, you can find the NVM repository here (https://github.com/nvm-sh/nvm).

- For Windows, a similar utility named "nvm-windows" is available. You can find it here (https://github.com/coreybutler/nvm-windows).

Even though we won't dive deep into NVM in this book, it's worth exploring as it can significantly streamline your Node.js development process.

Installing the Angular CLI

Once Node.js and npm are installed, you can install the Angular CLI globally on your system by running the following command in your terminal or command prompt:

```
npm install -g @angular/cli
```

Getting Help

Once installed, getting help is only a few keystrokes away.

```
ng help <command-name (Default: all)>
```

This command can be used to get general help or help on a specific ng command.

Starting a New Angular Project

This command creates a new directory and a new Angular app, for example, "ng new [name]".

```
ng new <options...>
```

Some of the more common options are

- `--dry-run (Boolean) (Default: false)` – Run through without making any changes.

- `--skip-install (Boolean) (Default: false)` – Skip installing packages.

- `--skip-git (Boolean) (Default: false)` – Skip initializing a git repository.

- `--standalone (Boolean) (Default: false)` – Creates an application based upon the standalone API, without NgModules.

- `--style (String) (Default: css)` – The style file default extension. Your choices are css, scss, sass, or less.

- `--prefix (String) (Default: app)` – The prefix to use for all component selectors.

- `--routing (Boolean) (Default: false)` – Generate a routing module.

If you run ng new without any parameters, the Angular CLI will walk you through everything.

Generating Project Assets

This command creates (generates) components, routes, services, interfaces, pipes, etc. with a simple command.

```
ng generate <blueprint> <options...>
```

By default, the CLI will also create simple test files for all of these. Available schematics:

- appShell
- application
- class
- component
- directive
- enum
- guard
- interceptor
- interface
- library
- module
- pipe
- service
- serviceWorker
- webWorker

Common Flags for Schematics

These flags are commonly used with most of the schematics:

- `--flat` (Boolean): Flag to indicate if a directory is created. By default, ng CLI will create a separate folder for most blueprints, even if there is only one file. If you know you won't be creating multiple files (templates, tests, etc.), you can pass true to this flag, and the CLI won't create the separate folder.

- `--spec` (Boolean): Specifies if a spec file is generated. Pass false to this flag to prevent the CLI from generating test files for you. Use this with caution. There are very few reasons not to have unit tests for your code.

- `--app` (String): Specifies app name to use.

- `--standalone` (Boolean): Specifies whether a component or directive should be created without an existing NgModule.

- `--module` (String): Allows specification of the declaring module. By default, the item being generated will be attached to the "closest containing module." The CLI will walk up the folder tree, looking for a module. Specifying a different module here will override that behavior.

There are other options available to many of these blueprints, further customizing their behavior.

Starting a Development Web Server

Builds and serves your app, rebuilding on file changes.

```
ng serve <options...>
```

When running ng serve, the compiled output is served from memory, not from disk. This means that the application being served is not located on disk in the dist folder. By default, ng serve will serve your application on http://localhost:4200. It will not, however, open a web browser for you. You can override these settings through the following options:

- --host (String): Allows you to change the host being served.

- --port (Number): Allows you to override the port served.

- --open: Causes the CLI to open your default browser automatically.

There are many other options available, but those three are probably the most common defaults you might want to override.

Checking Your Coding Style

Lints code in existing project. This command can be used to ensure that code style matches industry-standard practices, and can help keep your team's code styling consistent.

```
ng lint <options...>
```

One of the coolest options to ng lint is the --fix=true option. As its name implies, this option attempts to fix any linting errors it finds. Some of the more common fixes it can make are spacing issues, missing semicolons, consistent quoting types (single or double). I recommend you only run this option on a pristine git repository, making it easy to undo if it breaks something.

Running Unit Tests

Run unit tests in existing project.

```
ng test <options...>
```

The ng CLI sets up your tests by default unless you override that behavior. You don't have to spend your valuable time configuring your tests. If you use the ng CLI, they will be configured automatically.

Building Your Projects

Builds your app and places it into the output path (`dist/` by default).

```
ng build <options...>
```

Additional Commands

Here are some other commands that are used less often, included here for completeness:

- `ng doc <keyword>`: Opens the official Angular documentation for a given keyword.

- `ng e2e <options...>`: Run end-to-end (integration) tests in existing project.

- `ng version <options...>`: Outputs Angular CLI version.

- `ng xi18n <options...>`: Extracts i18n messages from source code.

Summary

In conclusion, the Angular CLI is a powerful and versatile tool that empowers developers to automate and streamline a wide range of tasks, from project creation to testing and deployment. It not only enhances productivity but also ensures consistency in code quality and style. For more comprehensive guidance and insights on utilizing the full potential of the Angular CLI, you can refer to the official documentation at Angular CLI (raw URL: `https://cli.angular.io/`).

CHAPTER 4

A Simple Angular Component

Embracing simplicity can often lead to powerful results, and Angular components are no exception. With just a dash of HTML and CSS, we can craft reusable components that can become the cornerstone of any project. This chapter will guide you through the process of creating one such universally applicable component – a "Loading" indicator.

In the realm of web development, one of the most common requirements is a visual indication of data being fetched from a remote service. A Loading indicator serves this purpose, subtly communicating to the user that their request is in progress and that the application is actively working to retrieve their data. Angular's robust framework makes the creation of such a component impressively straightforward.

So, let's delve into the intricacies of crafting a reusable Loading indicator with Angular, illustrating just how simple and effective component creation can be. You might find that Angular's simplicity and power make it a joy to work with, transforming even the most mundane tasks into engaging challenges.

As we progress through this journey, I encourage you to follow along in your code editor of choice. The beauty of coding is that it's accessible from a variety of platforms – be it Atom, Sublime, WebStorm, or any other tool that you're comfortable with. However, for the purpose of this guide, I'll be using Visual Studio Code (VS Code) and the Angular CLI that we

M. D. Callaghan, *Angular for Business*, https://doi.org/10.1007/978-1-4842-9609-7_4

installed in the previous chapter. VS Code provides an intuitive and user-friendly interface, while the Angular CLI makes it easy to create, manage, and build Angular applications. Remember, the goal is not just to read and understand, but also to get your hands dirty with actual code. There's no better way to learn than by doing.

Create a New Angular Application

Before we dive into creating our "Loading" component, we need an Angular application to house it. This is where the Angular CLI, installed in the previous chapter, comes into play. The CLI, or Command Line Interface, is a powerful tool that allows us to scaffold and manage Angular applications directly from the command line.

We'll start by creating a new Angular application. Open your terminal and navigate to the directory where you'd like to create your project. Then, type the following command:

```
ng new --standalone
```

This command asks the Angular CLI to create a new application with the standalone format introduced in Angular 15.2. Follow the prompts that appear after running this command to set up routing and select a stylesheet format. For the sample code in this book, using the Angular Router and CSS for styles will suffice. Once the process completes, you'll have a fresh Angular application ready for development.

Before you go any further, open the app.component.html file and remove its contents. Angular gives you a lot of content, but it'll just get in the way and confuse things. If you want to leave something like <h1>My Great App!</h1>, that's fine.

Navigate into your new project's directory using the command cd <app-name>. Now we're set up and ready to create our "Loading" component.

Create the Component

To create the component, I used the Angular CLI. I like to use the integrated terminal inside of VS Code, but use whatever you're comfortable with. Whatever you use, ensure that you are physically in the root folder of the application you just created.

```
npx ng generate component Loading --skip-tests --dry-run
CREATE src/app/loading/loading.component.scss (0 bytes)
CREATE src/app/loading/loading.component.html (22 bytes)
CREATE src/app/loading/loading.component.ts (301 bytes)
```

This command asks the Angular CLI to generate a new component named "Loading", not to bother generating a test file (I will explain why not shortly) and then simply show me what the command will do (–dry-run).

I almost always do a dry run before having the CLI generate anything for me. That way, I can see what files it will create and where it will put them. On some projects, I like to organize components differently than the default folders. Seeing the file paths before creation gives me a chance to correct them, simply by pre-pending the path to the name of the component.

In this case, I am comfortable with the component living in its own folder under app, so I can rerun the command without the –dry-run flag.

```
npx ng generate component Loading --skip-tests
CREATE src/app/loading/loading.component.scss (0 bytes)
CREATE src/app/loading/loading.component.html (22 bytes)
CREATE src/app/loading/loading.component.ts (301 bytes)
```

A note about the npx prefix: I need to add this to the command because my ng is not installed globally. Using npx causes the Angular CLI installed in my project's node_modules folder to be used. If your Angular CLI is installed globally, you can omit the npx prefix.

Component Code

This is the simplest part because there really is no logic to speak of. I am simply creating a visual component with no other behavior.

Inside the file loading.component.ts, the generated code looks like this:

```
import { Component } from "@angular/core";
import { CommonModule } from "@angular/common";

@Component({
  selector: "app-loading",
  standalone: true,
  imports: [CommonModule],
  templateUrl: "./loading.component.html",
  styleUrls: ["./loading.component.css"],
})
export class LoadingComponent {}
```

As I said, there is not much here. After the two imports is the @Component decorator, which defines how the component will be implemented. selector defines the custom component's HTML tag. This is how the component will be placed on a page.

```
<app-loading></app-loading>
```

You can also see that standalone is set to true, meaning we will not need an NgModule to use the component. Following that is the imports array, which we saw in the Gentle Introduction to Angular. Finally, the templateUrl and styleUrls are specified. These two lines tell the Angular compiler (and us) where to find the markup and styles for the component, respectively.

Next is the class body itself, which should be empty. We'll fix that now by adding two variables.

```
import { Component, Input } from "@angular/core";
import { CommonModule } from "@angular/common";

@Component({
  selector: "app-loading",
  standalone: true,
  imports: [CommonModule],
  templateUrl: "./loading.component.html",
  styleUrls: ["./loading.component.css"],
})
export class LoadingComponent {
  @Input() label = "";
  @Input() shown = false;
}
```

The @Input decorators tell Angular to expose those two variables as attributes on the custom HTML tag:

- label will be bound to some text in the HTML so that we can tell the user exactly what is loading. If you do not need that, you could eliminate it entirely.

- shown allows the host to show or hide the component as necessary. Something like this:

```
<app-loading label="Loading data now..." [shown]="isLoading">
</app-loading>
```

With this example markup, I have hard-coded the loading message, but have bound the shown attribute to a variable on the host component. Whenever isLoading is true in the host component, the loading component will be visible; otherwise it will be hidden. That is all the host needs to be concerned with. How the visibility is implemented inside the loading component is irrelevant to the host.

Markup

Now let us take a look at the markup. This, too, is pretty simple, almost trivial.

```
<div class="wrapper" [class.hidden]="!shown">
  <img src="./images/loading.gif" />
  <h1>Please Wait While We Complete Your Request</h1>
  <p>{{label}}</p>
</div>
```

The component consists of a single <div> with a class called wrapper, which I show in Figure 4-1. We will see more of that in the next section on styling. Inside this <div> are three more elements:

Figure 4-1. *Loading GIF from Pixabay.com*

- An `<img>` tag pointing at an animated gif. You can use any animated gif you'd like. I found a suitable one at pixabay.com (which I'll touch on in more detail later in the book. For reference, this is the image I used: Pixabay Image or `https://pixabay.com/gifs/load-loading-process-wait-delay-37`.

- The image is placed in an images folder just inside the loading component's folder. At build time, it will be copied to the correct place and referenced appropriately.

- A title represented by an `<h1>` tag containing a hard-coded message to the user.

- The final piece of content is a `<p>` tag with its text bound to the `@Input()` `label` field on the component. Whatever the host component passes as the label attribute will be displayed here.

Styling

The real magic happens in the component's stylesheet. I will show the entire thing, followed by an explanation of the relevant sections.

```
h1 {
  line-height: 30px;
  font-size: 24px;
}
.loader {
  width: 150px;
  height: 150px;
  display: inline-block;
```

```
    background-image: url(images/loading.gif);
    background-repeat: no-repeat;
    background-size: contain;
}

.hidden {
    display: none;
}

.wrapper {
    text-align: center;
    font-weight: 400;
    line-height: 18px;
    padding: 60px 20px 20px 20px;
    background-color: #ffffff;
    z-index: 9000;

    width: 480px;
    height: 326px;

    position: absolute;
    top: 50%;
    left: 50%;
    transform: translate(-50%, -50%);

    outline: 9999px solid rgba(217, 217, 217, 0.75);
}
```

h1

The first rule is for the <h1> tag, and it is pretty straightforward. It simply sets the font-size to 30px, and the line-height to a slightly lower value. These values do not materially change the component. They are purely aesthetic and you could change them to reflect your own personal style. One thing of note is that the Loading Component will inherit its host's font selection, whatever that may be.

.div.loader

The elements with the class `.loader` have a width and height of 150 pixels, and are displayed as inline-block. They have a background image set to images/loading.gif, with no repeating and a background size set to contain. This is the animated gif. INSERT IMAGE HERE One of the little bits of "magic" that Angular does for us is that it will ensure that the image referenced in the CSS file will be copied to the right place at build time and the CSS references updated as needed.

.hidden

The component's visibility is driven by this class. The wrapping `<div>` either does or does not have this class set, based on the value of the shown attribute.

Why did I not put the hidden class on the host and let the host handle it directly? The reason I wanted to use shown is so that I could change the visibility implementation at will, without changing any of the host code. For example, I could add some CSS animation or implement some other complex code, all without the host components even knowing about it. They would continue to set `[shown]` as they do now.

.wrapper

This is the big one, so I will show the code again for convenience, explaining it as I go.

```
text-align: center;
font-weight: 400;
line-height: 18px;
padding: 60px 20px 20px 20px;
background-color: #ffffff;
z-index: 9000;
```

You can see some various rules that dictate how the component looks. The first line indicates that everything inside the wrapper will be centered, text and images both. The next three lines set the text font-weight to 400 (normal), a default line-height of 18px, and some internal padding to provide whitespace.

It has a background color of white, indicated by the value #ffffff.

The z-index of 9000 is a relative position of depth. Elements with larger numbers appear "on top of" or "in front of" elements with a z-index value that is smaller. Setting the loading component's z-index to 9000 gives it a decent likelihood that no other elements will appear in front of it. Should you find that is not the case, set a higher value. Browsers do not seem to have a standard "maximum" value, but most modern browsers should allow values up to $(2^{31} - 1)$.

```
width: 480px;
height: 326px;
```

These two values simply set a fixed width and height for the component. We could be clever and specify values in terms of window or viewport size, but I wanted to keep this part simple. Feel free to experiment with different values. That's what source control is for, right?

```
position: absolute;
top: 50%;
left: 50%;
transform: translate(-50%, -50%);
```

This next block helps to position the loading component. The combination of positioning the element at top: 50% and left: 50%, along with the transform: translate(-50%, -50%) property, is commonly used to center an element horizontally and vertically.

Setting top: 50% and left: 50% positions the element's top-left corner at the exact center of its parent container. However, this alone would not center the element perfectly, as it would be offset by half of its own width and height.

That's where the translate(-50%, -50%) comes into play. It moves the element back by 50% of its own width and height in both the horizontal and vertical directions. This effectively centers the element perfectly, regardless of its size.

By combining these positioning and transformation properties, you achieve a consistent and reliable way to center an element both horizontally and vertically.

```
outline: 9999px solid rgba(217, 217, 217, 0.75);
```

The clever bit I find is the last line: outline. The component's outline is being defined as a 75% opaque (i.e., 25% transparent) solid gray line 9999px wide. This ends up covering the entire host component with the outline, preventing it from being selectable.

And that is the entire component!

Use

I hinted at its use previously, but there are three things you would need to use it in your own project.

- Include the source files.

- Import the component in the host's components imports array.

- Supply some HTML markup to call it, which looks like this.

```
<app-loading [label]="loadingText" [shown]="isLoading">
</app-loading>
```

In this sample code, I am using Angular's attribute binding syntax to bind the label and shown attributes to the host component's loadingText and isLoading variables, respectively. Changes to these variables on the host component will cause Angular to re-render the loading component as necessary.

If you are following along, you should be able to drop the component right onto the app.component.html page, like this:

```
<h1>My Great App!</h1>

<button (click)="load()">Toggle Loading</button>

<app-loading label="Loading data now..." [shown]="isLoading">
</app-loading>
```

In addition to the <h1> element displaying the text "My Great App!", you can see I've added a <button> element with the label "Toggle Loading", and an <app-loading> component that shows a loading message when the isLoading variable is true.

To set that isLoading variable, all you need to do is add that load() function inside of app.component.ts. One possible implementation could be:

```
load() {
  this.isLoading = true;
  setTimeout(() => {
    this.isLoading = false;
  }, 2500);
}
```

The load function will set the isLoading property to true, which will trigger the display of the loading component. After a delay of 2500 milliseconds, the isLoading property will be set to false, hiding the loading component.

The Result

Start the Angular server by typing ng serve or npm start at the command line. You should end up with something like Figure 4-2.

Figure 4-2. *Loading toggle button*

When you click the button, you'll see the component in action, as shown in Figure 4-3.

Figure 4-3. *Visibile loading indicator*

Summary

In this chapter, we've debunked the notion that Angular components have to be complex. We've demonstrated that, with minimal HTML and CSS, it's entirely possible to craft a reusable "Loading" component. This component, with its simple yet efficient functionality, can be easily incorporated into any part of our application, enhancing the user experience whenever data is being fetched.

Moreover, with a bit more tweaking and refinement, we can evolve this component into a standalone entity. Such a standalone component, decoupled from specific project dependencies, could be a versatile tool in your development toolkit, ready to be dropped into any Angular project you work on.

But where could we use such a component? That's what we'll explore in our next chapter. We'll delve into practical applications for our "Loading" component and see how it can enhance the interactivity and responsiveness of our applications. So, stay tuned, and let's continue this journey of learning and discovery together. As always, I welcome your thoughts and suggestions on how we can improve and optimize this component further.

CHAPTER 5

Guardians of the [Angular] Galaxy

As we journey deeper into Angular, we uncover more powerful tools that not only enhance the functionality of our applications but also secure their operation. One such tool is the Route Guard. Route Guards act as gatekeepers, deciding whether navigation to a requested route is permissible or should be blocked.

In this chapter, we'll take a look at them and review a simple implementation. So, let's dive in and meet these Guardians of the Routes!

Understanding Angular Route Guards

Angular Route Guards are functions which tell the Angular router to allow or deny navigation to a requested route. They act as security checkpoints, controlling whether a user can navigate to or away from a certain route. Route Guards are a powerful tool to add an extra layer of protection and control to your Angular applications.

Angular offers several built-in guard types like `CanActivate`, `CanDeactivate`, `CanLoad`, and `Resolve`, each serving a specific purpose in the navigation life cycle. These guards can be used to implement complex scenarios such as user authentication, role-based access control, and form-change confirmation.

The Value Proposition of Guards

The Angular Route Guard comes with a suite of benefits:

- User access control: Guards can be used to control which users have access to certain routes based on their roles or permissions.

- Data protection: They can protect data on a page from being lost when the user navigates away.

- Load optimization: They can prevent lazy-loaded modules from loading until certain conditions are met.

- Data pre-fetching: Guards can fetch the data required for a specific route in advance using `Resolve` guards. We'll look more at the resolver later.

In this chapter, I'll focus on `CanActivate`. I'll talk about `Resolver` guards in the next chapter.

Practical Application of Guards

To see how Angular Route Guards work in a real-world application, let's create a Guard that checks if a date parameter in a route is valid and not in the past.

```
export dateGuard: CanActivateFn = (route, state) => {
    const dateParam = route.params['date'];
    const date = new Date(dateParam);

    if (!isNaN(date.getTime()) && date > new Date()) {
      return true;
    } else {
      alert('Invalid or past date!');
```

```
      return false;
    }
  }
```

Notice that dateGuard is a function instead of a class. This is an example of a functional route guard.

It takes two parameters: route, an instance of ActivatedRouteSnapshot, and state, an instance of RouterStateSnapshot. The function can return an Observable, Promise, a boolean, or a UrlTree.

- If all guards return true, the navigation continues.

- If any guard returns false, the navigation is canceled.

- If any guard returns a UrlTree, the current navigation is canceled, and a new navigation begins to the UrlTree returned from the guard.

The dateGuard in the preceding code is a simple implementation of the CanActivateFn function definition.

This function verifies that the "date" route parameter is valid and not in the past. If the date isn't valid or is in the past, an alert is shown to the user, and navigation to the route is not allowed.

The guard is then applied to a route in the route configuration:

```
import { dateGuard } from "./date.guard";

const routes: Routes = [
  {
    path: "event/:date",
    component: EventComponent,
    canActivate: [dateGuard],
  },
];
```

In this case, the EventComponent is activated only if the "date" parameter in the route is a valid date and is not in the past.

Beyond Parameter Validation

While the previous example focuses on parameter validation, Angular Route Guards can also be used for complex security applications like user authentication and role-based access control. In these scenarios, the guard checks a user's authentication status or roles to determine whether they should be allowed to navigate to a certain route.

Although the guard's internal logic and complexity may vary, the fundamental mechanism remains the same: analyzing the situation (e.g., checking parameters or a user's authenticated state) and making a decision about whether or not to allow navigation.

Here's a basic implementation of an authentication guard:

```
export authGuard: CanActivateFn = (route, state) => {
  authService = inject(AuthService);

  if (this.authService.isAuthenticated()) {
    return true;
  } else {
    console.log("Not authenticated, redirecting...");
    this.authService.redirectToLogin();
    return false;
  }
}
```

In this example, the guard checks if the user is authenticated by calling isAuthenticated() on an AuthService. If the user is authenticated, it returns true and navigation proceeds. If not, it redirects the user to a login page and returns false, stopping the navigation.

Alternatively, we could have the guard return a `UrlTree` to a login page instead, which would cause the Angular Router to redirect the user to that page.

The `inject` Function

You may have noticed another new function in that preceding code. It is worth a brief discussion.

Traditional constructor injection in Angular is a method where dependencies are supplied directly into a class's constructor. The dependencies required by a class are declared as constructor parameters, and Angular's DI system takes care of instantiating and providing those dependencies when the class is created. Here's a brief example of what this might look like:

```
@Injectable()
export class Car {
  constructor(private engine: Engine) {}
}
```

In this traditional approach, the DI system identifies the `Engine` dependency based on the type annotation in the constructor and injects an appropriate instance.

The `inject` function, on the other hand, provides an alternative way to acquire dependencies within an injection context. It can be used not only in the constructor but also in field initializers and specific factory functions, called *injection contexts*. Here's how you could utilize the `inject` function:

```
@Injectable({ providedIn: "root" })
export class Car {
  radio: Radio = inject(Radio);
  spareTire = inject(Tire);

  // Empty constructor no longer required
}
```

The key differences between traditional constructor injection and using the inject function include

- Usage beyond constructors: Unlike constructor injection, where dependencies are only injected through the constructor parameters, inject allows for the manual injection of dependencies even in property initializations.

- Explicit injection: The inject function offers a more explicit way to request dependencies, giving you the option to inject a dependency where needed, rather than solely at the construction phase.

Injection Context

The injection context refers to the specific situation or place where the inject function can be utilized. It is essential to adhere to the injection context because calling the inject function outside of it will result in an error. This context ensures that dependencies are provided consistently and only when appropriate, maintaining the integrity of the application's architecture.

For example, calling `inject` within the lifecycle hooks like `ngOnInit` is disallowed, as it is considered outside the valid injection context. This context-awareness guarantees that dependencies are only injected at suitable points, thus avoiding potential conflicts or unexpected behaviors in the application.

In summary, the `inject` function offers a flexible, powerful alternative to constructor injection, with clear benefits in terms of control, code conciseness, and error management. Understanding and adhering to the injection context is critical to utilizing this function effectively within the application's design.

Summary

Angular Route Guards are an indispensable tool for Angular developers, providing powerful control over access and navigation within an application. By utilizing their capabilities, developers can ensure the right data is shown to the right user at the right time, enhancing both data security and user experience. In the next chapter, we will delve into more complex guard use cases and also explore how to handle redirection when a guard prevents navigation.

CHAPTER 6

Resolve or Die: Error Handling Strategies for Loading Data

Angular Route Guards and Resolvers

Angular provides a powerful mechanism for controlling access to routes in your application – Route Guards. These sentinel-like entities effectively ensure that certain conditions are met before a route is activated. Are you wondering if a user is authenticated? A Route Guard can verify that. If the user isn't authenticated or doesn't belong to the appropriate authorization group, access to the guarded route is denied. Route Guards embody the Single Responsibility Principle, are easily mockable for unit tests, and significantly enhance the security of your application. But this raises a question – where do Route Resolvers fit into this picture?

Let's explore Route Resolvers. Similar to Route Guards, Route Resolvers serve as gatekeepers, but with a nuanced difference. Rather than preventing the user from accessing a page, a Resolver ensures that certain preconditions are met before the route is fully activated. Typically, Resolvers preload necessary data for a page before it renders.

© Michael D. Callaghan 2024
M. D. Callaghan, *Angular for Business*, https://doi.org/10.1007/978-1-4842-9609-7_6

Consider a scenario where you have a page showing order status to the user. The route might look something like this: /orderstatus/:orderId. A Route Guard would verify that the logged-in user is associated with the requested order. That's the straightforward part, but what about a Route Resolver? Should you also ensure that the order details are preloaded before the page displays? The answer, as we'll see, isn't black and white – it depends. Let's dive deeper and explore these crucial concepts.

What Data Are You Loading?

In the previous scenario, you need to load the order details: what items are on the order, which of those items have been shipped or on back-order, and the tracking information for the items that have been shipped. There may be other details your system has to load. Maybe the item descriptions and payment information come from other systems, and you want to display those, too. The questions you need to ask yourself are which data items are so important that you will not even want to display the page without them? And what if you cannot load those items?

The answer to the first question is really an application design decision. Do you want to ensure that all the order details have been successfully loaded before the Order Status Page appears? Or is it acceptable to render the page partially, and allow the order details to appear as its data is returned? If the order status typically takes less than a second to load completely, waiting for it might be acceptable.

What If There Are Errors?

Depending on which pattern you choose, you then need to decide what to do if one or more pieces of data cannot be loaded. A service could be down, the network could be flaky, etc. It really does not matter. What do you do?

Give Up on Error

If you are using a Route Resolver, and it encounters an unhandled exception, the route will not resolve, and your page will simply not render. This is obviously not ideal, and you should throw out this idea immediately.

You could catch and log the error, setting the data being loaded to an empty or default object, and then letting the resolver complete successfully. If you do that, you need to think of what the rendered page would look like. Is it still useful for the person trying to load the page? If the answer is yes, then perhaps this is an acceptable solution. You can actually make this choice a case-by-case decision, based on the importance of data being loaded. If it is not "mission critical", go ahead and let the page load.

Redirect to an Error Page

On the other hand, maybe your data is so critical that not a smidgen of the page should appear until it is all available. If any missing piece of data causes the page to be useless, consider redirecting to an error page with an explanation of what went wrong. You could optionally provide a link on the error page, allowing the user to retry. After all, it may have been a temporary blip.

Here is some sample code that illustrates one way to redirect to an error page if any errors are encountered in the Resolver. The primary advantage to this method is that the page itself need not be modified, or even know about the resolver. If the component loads, you can be sure that the data is there. Thus, the code I am showing here is the resolver itself, and I am not showing the page component.

The Resolver shown in the following is an example of Angular's functional resolver. The class-based resolvers have been deprecated and will be removed from Angular soon.

```
export const dataResolverResolver: ResolveFn<boolean> = (route,
state) => {
  const dataService = inject(DataService);
  const router = inject(Router);

  dataService.getData().pipe(
    map((data) => {
      // Here we would do something with the data
    }),
    catchError((error) => {
      router.navigateByUrl("/error");
      throw error;
    })
  );
  return true;
};
```

Maybe Not Use a Resolver

Going back to the Order Status scenario, imagine that there is really only one piece of data that would make the entire page useless. And even then, if the page renders without this data, and instead displays an inline error, what is the ultimate harm?

Allow me to suggest another option. Consider not using a Route Resolver at all.

Loading Indicator

A common pattern I am sure you have seen is to render the complete page, but with no data. The page displays a "Loading" indicator of some sort while the order details are retrieved, with the page in a non-interactive state. Once the details are available, the indicator disappears and the user can interact with the page at that point. This is a pretty common pattern, which we have all seen.

Here is some sample code that implements this pattern, using the loading indicator from the last chapter.

The getData() function is asynchronous so that it can use promises. I would normally use RxJS throughout my code, but I didn't want it to get in the way of what we're discussing here.

```
export class LoadingExampleComponent implements OnInit {
  errorText = "";
  isLoading = false;
  data = "";

  // Alternative service injection
  // dataService = inject(DataService);

  constructor(private dataService: DataService) {}

  ngOnInit() {
    this.getData();
  }

  async getData() {
    this.errorText = "";
    this.isLoading = true;
```

```
try {
  this.data = await firstValueFrom(this.dataService.
  getData());
} catch (error: any) {
  this.errorText = error.message;
} finally {
  this.isLoading = false;
}
}
}
```

And this is some markup that would go with it. The error message <p>
tag, including the retry link, is only displayed if the string is not empty.

```
<p>Data from service: {{ data }}</p>
<p *ngIf="errorText">Error: {{ errorText }}. You can <a
(click)="getData()">retry</a>, or <a href="/home">return
home</a>.</p>
<app-loading label="Loading data now..." [shown]="isLoading">
</app-loading>
```

Skeleton Text

Yet another pattern renders the page with skeleton text, gray text bars
in place of where the details will eventually appear. The page is fully
interactive, giving the impression of faster performance, while the other
details load. As the data is loaded successfully, it replaces the skeleton text.
Any piece of data that fails to load could be replaced with an error message
and a retry link.

For this demo, I selected the ngx-skeleton-loader from npmjs (www.
npmjs.com/package/ngx-skeleton-loader).

Here is some sample code to implement this pattern. It is mostly the same, with very minimal UI changes. I find this pattern to be a lot cleaner, because the error message and skeleton text visibility are both managed entirely by the view layer (i.e., the HTML).

There is more markup than in the prior example, primarily due to the inclusion of the skeleton text. The method of displaying the error and retry link is identical. However, the skeleton text is hidden as soon as either the data or the error message has a value.

```html
<div *ngIf="errorText && !isLoading">
  <h1>Error</h1>
  <p>{{ errorText }}</p>
</div>
<div *ngIf="isLoading">
  <h1>
    <ngx-skeleton-loader></ngx-skeleton-loader>
  </h1>
  <p>
    <ngx-skeleton-loader [count]="3"></ngx-skeleton-loader>
  </p>
</div>
```

Either of these alternative patterns can be handled by kicking off the data load by clicking a button or during ngOnInit, calling into the same data service the Route Resolver would call. This strategy maintains a proper separation of concerns, and allows the service to be mocked during testing.

Demo

Here is a demo I created with the preceding code to show all three of these options side-by-side. The demo consists of three Angular page components, each attempting to load some data from a common service, as you can see in Figure 6-1. The service simply waits 3.5 seconds and throws an error, as shown in Figure 6-2.

Loading

Figure 6-1. *Loading text*

Error State

Resolve or Die

This demo shows various options for handling errors when loading data. Click the button to simulate a request. The loading component will be shown for about 2.5 seconds, and then will error out.

| Get Data |

Error	Error	Error
This is a fake error	This is a fake error	This is a fake error

Resolver w/Error Page   Loading Indicator   Skeleton Text

Figure 6-2. *Error state*

If you wish to see the demo code in its entirety, please see the GitHub repo included with the book's extras.

Note, I used a different "loading" indicator because the one we wrote in the last chapter takes up the whole page. Feel free to swap it out for that one as an exercise if you wish.

Summary

I wrote this in response to a real situation I had in a recent project. The main page needed four different pieces of data, all loaded from separate sources. The implementation used a Route Resolver to ensure all the data loaded before the page appeared. During testing, one of the services was down and was timing out after 30 seconds. This means the user was kept staring at a white screen until the service gave up. Obviously, this experience is not ideal, and led me to research other (better?) options.

As part of that research, I came up with some guidelines for deciding how best to load asynchronous data:

- If your page absolutely cannot be shown unless/until all data is loaded, use a resolver.

- Do not ignore errors in your resolver, or your page will not render and the user will be stuck in limbo.

- Redirect the user to an error page, optionally with a retry button.

- If your page is still somewhat useful with partial data, load the data asynchronously in ngOnInit.

- Use skeleton text or a loading indicator.

Try all the options yourself to see how each one behaves and choose the option that works best for your projects.

CHAPTER 7

Custom Angular Checkbox with [(ngModel)] Support

Recently, I needed to add some custom styles to a checkbox in an Angular app. I found a simple example of what I wanted to do, implemented entirely with CSS and HTML, and containing no imperative code. Delighted with this discovery, I copied the CSS into my page and got it working with a few tweaks. Then I wondered what it would take to turn it into a custom component I could reuse. As it turns out, it was harder than I thought, but not overwhelming. The solution is described here.

Custom-Styled Checkbox

The UI design I was trying to copy required a custom-styled checkbox. This one needed a fat white check mark inside a green box when checked, and an empty gray square when unchecked. Further, the design called for the checkbox control itself to be larger than normal and had a specific requirement for the label's spacing.

M. D. Callaghan, *Angular for Business*, https://doi.org/10.1007/978-1-4842-9609-7_7

CSS

I will start by showing the final CSS in case you want to follow along, but I will not be describing the styles. The point of this post is to show the Angular component. If you want a more complete explanation of the styling, this is where I got the HTML and CSS I used: W3School (`www.w3schools.com`). I tweaked their CSS a bit, but not by much.

```css
:host {
  display: block;

  /* The container */
  .cb-container {
    display: inline-block;
    position: relative;
    padding-left: 30px;
    margin-bottom: 12px;
    cursor: pointer;
    -webkit-user-select: none;
    -moz-user-select: none;
    -ms-user-select: none;
    user-select: none;
    line-height: 22px;
  }

  /* Hide the browser's default checkbox */
  .cb-container input {
    position: absolute;
    opacity: 0;
    cursor: pointer;
    height: 0;
    width: 0;
  }
```

```css
/* Create a custom checkbox */
.checkmark {
  position: absolute;
  top: 0;
  left: 0;
  height: 20px;
  width: 20px;
  background-color: #ffffff;
  border: 1px solid #00aa00;
  border-radius: 2px;
}

/* On mouse-over, add a grey background color */
.cb-container:hover input ~ .checkmark {
  background-color: #ffffff;
}

/* When the checkbox is checked, add a green background */
.cb-container input:checked ~ .checkmark {
  background-color: #00aa00;
  border-color: #00aa00;
}

/* Create the checkmark/indicator (hidden when not
checked) */
.checkmark:after {
  content: "";
  position: absolute;
  display: none;
}
```

```css
/* Show the checkmark when checked */
.cb-container input:checked ~ .checkmark:after {
  display: block;
}

/* Style the checkmark/indicator */
.cb-container .checkmark:after {
  left: 6px;
  top: 0px;
  width: 7px;
  height: 17px;
  border: solid white;
  border-width: 0 4px 4px 0;
  -webkit-transform: rotate(45deg);
  -ms-transform: rotate(45deg);
  transform: rotate(45deg);
}

.cb-container.disabled {
  cursor: not-allowed;
  pointer-events: none;
  opacity: 0.5;
  }
}
```

my-checkbox.component.css

The Component

With the checkbox styled the way I wanted it, my next thought was that
I should bundle it as an Angular component so that I could reuse it on
other pages. Then I realized that the UX design required that the checkbox
label should always be on the right, the same size, and the same distance

from the box. At that point, it really sounds more and more like a custom component. And since I am now thinking of a custom component, I should see about making it work with [(ngModel)].

Here is how I envisioned the custom checkbox component would be used.

```
<app-checkbox text="Remember Me" [disabled]="!isLoggedIn"
[(ngModel)]="remember"> </app-checkbox>
```

This means I needed a way to pass in a string to be used for the label, a boolean to set the disabled property, and 2-way binding for the value of the checkbox itself. The first two were pretty easy. The third required some custom Angular code.

Create the Component

The first order of business is to create the component, with the help of the Angular CLI.

```
ng generate component MyCheckbox --standalone --skip-tests=true
CREATE src/app/my-checkbox/my-checkbox.component.css (0 bytes)
CREATE src/app/my-checkbox/my-checkbox.component.html
(26 bytes)
CREATE src/app/my-checkbox/my-checkbox.component.ts (316 bytes)
```

The component has no business logic to speak of, so I skipped tests. I may regret that later, but it will do for now. This command created the three files listed previously. As I have been doing with all components since Angular 15.2, I created it as "standalone," without an NgModule. Any other pages or components that want to include MyCheckboxComponent need to import it directly, as you'll see shortly.

Add the HTML Template

Next, I needed to add the modest HTML to the newly-created component. Here is the HTML:

```
<label class="cb-container" [class.disabled]="disabled">
  {{ text }}
  <input type="checkbox" [checked]="isChecked"
(change)="onChanged($event)" (blur)="onBlur($event)"
[disabled]="disabled" />
  <span class="checkmark"></span>
</label>
```

The `<label>` element serves as the container for the checkbox. The fact that it wraps the input means that someone can click on the label to check and uncheck the checkbox. Inside the label, there is a placeholder for text that will be replaced with a value from the component. The `<input>` element with the type "checkbox" represents the checkbox itself. It has some important attributes:

- The checked attribute determines whether the checkbox is checked, based on a value from the component.

- The change event handler triggers a method in the component when the checkbox value changes. We'll hook into this soon.

- The blur event triggers a method in the Angular component when the checkbox loses focus. As you'll see this will be important soon.

- The disabled attribute does what you'd expect: disables the checkbox based on a value from the component. Unsurprisingly, if set to a "truthy" value, this will cause

the checkbox to be disabled. The <span> element with
the class "checkmark" represents the visual indicator
for the checkbox.

Component Fields

With the HTML template complete, the next step is to create the fields and
functions referred to. I added the two fields at the top of the component's
class, and the event handler after the constructor.

```
@Input() text = '';
@Input() disabled = false;
```

Both fields are annotated with Angular's @Input decorator, which
is what enables their values to be specified from the parent component,
using standard HTML syntax.

```
onChanged($event: Event) {
  const isChecked = ($event.target as HTMLInputElement)?.
  checked;
  this.isChecked = isChecked;
}
```

The onChanged function is called whenever the <input> changes (in
other words, the checkbox is checked or cleared). The $event parameter is
a standard HTML DOM Event object. It is in this function where I manually
set the isChecked field to either true or false, based on the actual state of
the checkbox. I am being overly paranoid by casting the event target to an
HTMLInputElement and ensuring that it is "truthy" before retrieving the
checked attribute. It may be paranoid, but it works.

No Value Accessor

At this point, there is a custom checkbox that can be dropped inside any other component.

<app-my-checkbox text="Remember me" **disabled**="false" **/>**

It will work, except for two things:

- The host container will not be able to get the state of the checkbox at runtime.

- The [(ngModel)] attribute cannot be used. If it is, you will get a nasty error at runtime that there is "No Value Accessor" on the component.

Fortunately, these two problems share a common solution. The custom component needs to implement Angular's ControlValueAccessor interface.

ControlValueAccessor

If you look up this interface, you will find that it consists of four functions, each of which will need to be implemented on the component. We will look at those functions one by one.

writeValue( )

This function is called by Angular whenever a value change is being made from the hosting component. All you need to do is handle the value being passed in. Here, I am simply storing it, which incidentally changes the checkbox state, due to its internal data binding.

```
writeValue(obj: boolean): void {
  this.isChecked = obj;
}
```

registerOnChange()

This function is called by Angular to provide a callback function that the component needs to call whenever a change has occurred.

```
onChange = (_) => {}; // No-op
registerOnChange(fn: any): void {
  // Replace internal function with the one provided
  this.onChange = fn;
}
```

The pattern I am following here is to create a default onChange function on the component, which does absolutely nothing. Then when Angular calls registerOnChange, the component's onChange function is replaced with the callback function provided.

However, that is only half of the story. The custom component needs to call it, which happens in the onChanged function that is bound to the checkbox. For this, the component simply calls the internal onChange function, which should be the callback registered by Angular. If no callback has been registered, the default no-op function is called. This prevents the need for an "is null guard."

```
onChanged($event: Event) {
  const isChecked = ($event.target as HTMLInputElement)?.
  checked;
  this.isChecked = isChecked;
  this.onChange(isChecked);
}
```

registerOnTouched( )

This one is a little more obscure, and it doesn't seem to be necessary for a checkbox control. According to the official documentation:

> When implementing registerOnTouched in your own value accessor, save the given function so your class calls it when the control should be considered blurred or "touched".

This should not be confused with a mobile device's concept of "touched." Instead, it refers to a form having been touched or modified. In this custom component, I have wired up the checkbox's blur event. The pattern is the same as with registerOnChange().

```
onBlur = (_) => {}; // No-op

registerOnTouched(fn: any): void {
  // Call the parent's registered onTouched function, if any.
  // This lets it know that the checkbox lost focus.
  this.onBlur = fn;
}
```

setDisabledState( )

This function does what you might think: It is called by the forms API when the custom component should be disabled. In this case, I am setting an internal isDisabled field to whatever boolean value is provided. This value is then reflected on the component through data binding, and the checkbox is enabled or disabled appropriately.

```
setDisabledState?(isDisabled: boolean): void {
  this.disabled = isDisabled;
}
```

In the case of a checkbox, it is all pretty straightforward. You could also imagine a more complex control, which might consist of multiple input elements that can each be disabled. Angular Forms sees the custom component as a single control. When it disables that control, individual internal elements might need to be disabled according to different rules. Exactly how you handle that in your own controls is up to you.

I added a little CSS to set the opacity to 50% when disabled.

Registering the Provider

There is one last piece to getting everything to work happily together. The code inside the custom component is complete, but Angular still knows nothing about it. The solution has changed since Angular was released, and I found multiple solutions that no longer work. This example was tested on Angular 8 through 16.

The final step to register the custom component is to have the component provide the NG_VALUE_ACCESSOR inside the providers array inside its @Component decorator, as shown here:

```
providers: [
  {
    provide: NG_VALUE_ACCESSOR,
    useExisting: forwardRef(() => MyCheckboxComponent),
    multi: true,
  },
];
```

This code indicates to Angular that the component provides its own NG_VALUE_ACCESSOR, using an existing component. The catch-22 here is that the component has not yet been defined. Angular allows this through the use of the forwardRef function. Basically, it tells the dependency injection system that the component provided is yet to be defined but will be available at runtime. The parameter to the forwardRef function is an arrow function that returns the custom component's class.

The last property, `multi: true`, indicates that there may be more than one NG_VALUE_ACCESSORs being provided to the application, potentially from multiple places. It is enough to remember to set it to true.

Wrapping Up

At this point, the custom checkbox component is ready to be dropped onto any other page or component in the application. Because it was defined in a custom module, any other component wanting to use it would need to import that module into its own module (or the app's module).

As shown previously, here is a complete example of using this custom component inside of another component.

```
<app-my-checkbox [(ngModel)]="isChecked" [text]="text"
[disabled]="isDisabled" />
```

As you can see, it took a little bit of effort, but the result is that [(ngModel)] now simply "just works," which was the goal. Finally, because the component is recognized by Angular as a form control, it can be added to a Reactive Form, complete with custom validation rules, should you so desire.

The Complete Component

As a convenience, here is the complete component:

```
import { Component, Input, forwardRef } from "@angular/core";
import { ControlValueAccessor, NG_VALUE_ACCESSOR } from
"@angular/forms";
```

```
@Component({
  selector: "app-my-checkbox",
  templateUrl: "./my-checkbox.component.html",
  styleUrls: ["./my-checkbox.component.css"],
  standalone: true,
  providers: [
    {
      provide: NG_VALUE_ACCESSOR,
      useExisting: forwardRef(() => MyCheckboxComponent),
      multi: true,
    },
  ],
})
export class MyCheckboxComponent implements
ControlValueAccessor {
  // Bindable properties
  @Input() text = "";
  @Input() disabled = false;

  // Internal properties
  isChecked = false;

  onChange = (_: unknown) => {};
  onBlur = (_: unknown) => {};

  writeValue(obj: boolean): void {
    this.isChecked = obj;
  }

  registerOnChange(fn: any): void {
    this.onChange = fn;
  }
```

```
registerOnTouched(fn: any): void {
  this.onBlur = fn;
}

setDisabledState?(isDisabled: boolean): void {
  this.disabled = isDisabled;
}

onChanged($event: Event) {
  const isChecked = ($event.target as HTMLInputElement)?.
  checked;
  this.isChecked = isChecked;
  this.onChange(isChecked);
}
}
```

Filename: my-checkbox.component.ts

And the Template

```
<label class="cb-container" [class.disabled]="disabled">
  {{ text }}
  <input type="checkbox" [checked]="isChecked"
  (change)="onChanged($event)" (blur)="onBlur($event)"
  [disabled]="disabled" />
  <span class="checkmark"></span>
</label>
```

Filename: my-checkbox.component.html

You saw the CSS at the beginning of the chapter, so I won't reproduce it here.

Summary

In this chapter, we took a journey through the creation and customization of a checkbox in an Angular app, turning an ordinary HTML and CSS example into a reusable Angular component.

As we move forward, keep in mind the principles we've learned here – reusable components can significantly enhance both the developer experience and the user interface.

Looking ahead, I encourage you to experiment with adding this custom checkbox component to a Template or Reactive Form. Happy coding!

For More Information

- Angular Docs for the ControlValueAccessor: Angular Docs (`https://angular.io/api/forms/ ControlValueAccessor`)

- W3School Custom Checkbox: W3Schools Tutorial (`www.w3schools.com/howto/howto_css_custom_ checkbox.asp`)

- HTML DOM Event object: HTML DOM Event (`www. w3schools.com/jsref/dom_obj_event.asp`)

CHAPTER 8

Upgrading Angular

Maintaining your applications' compatibility with the latest Angular versions is a crucial responsibility for any team working with this robust platform. Angular adheres to a six-month release cycle, making it necessary to continually update your projects. As of this writing, Angular versions 12 and older are already unsupported. This means that these versions no longer receive official patches, bug fixes, or security updates from the Angular team. Using these unsupported versions for a critical project could expose your application to potential security vulnerabilities and degrade the overall quality of your codebase due to unresolved bugs.

Updating your Angular version not only mitigates these risks but also provides several benefits. These include gaining access to the latest features and improvements, performance enhancements, and the most recent security updates. Being on the cutting edge of Angular's technology can streamline your development process, facilitate better code practices, and create a more robust and secure application.

However, staying current with Angular updates can seem daunting, especially given the fear of breaking existing functionalities in the upgrade process. Fortunately, the Angular team has made significant strides in simplifying the update process, providing comprehensive guidance and tools to help developers migrate their projects safely and efficiently. By staying in tune with these updates, you'll ensure your applications remain robust, secure, and aligned with the best practices in the ever-evolving Angular ecosystem.

M. D. Callaghan, *Angular for Business*, https://doi.org/10.1007/978-1-4842-9609-7_8

Keep on Top of Things

The key to a smooth transition between Angular versions lies in regular, timely updates. Letting your project fall too far behind in versions can complicate the update process significantly. For instance, upgrading a project from Angular 5 directly to version 16 can be a complex and potentially risky operation. Instead, the best practice is to keep your project current or no more than two versions behind the latest release (n-2).

Angular's team prioritizes backward compatibility, meaning that most updates don't introduce breaking changes. When there is a need for such changes, the Angular team typically provides two to three versions' worth of advance warning. They use this time to highlight the upcoming changes, often deprecating the soon-to-be-obsolete features but keeping them functional until the scheduled removal. This procedure affords developers the time to adapt their codebases progressively, reducing the risk of an abrupt and potentially detrimental change.

Therefore, adopting a regular update schedule helps ensure that these transitions are not overwhelming. Regularly updating Angular versions as they're released makes each upgrade a minor task, rather than a monumental effort. This approach allows your team to incorporate the latest features, fixes, and improvements into your project continually, enhancing the overall performance and stability of your applications.

Staying on top of Angular's updates is a manageable task when you don't allow your project to lag too far behind. By doing so, you can leverage the latest improvements while ensuring your applications remain robust, secure, and compliant with modern development best practices.

Follow Along

You can utilize the very same steps outlined in this chapter to upgrade your own Angular projects. Bear in mind, the procedure will remain similar regardless of the specific versions you are migrating between. We'll be demonstrating an upgrade from version 12 to 16 – spanning four major releases – which may represent the most ambitious leap you'd want to undertake in a single stride without conducting extensive and meticulous testing.

Remember, each version change may introduce changes that could potentially affect your project. Therefore, although the steps are similar across versions, it's important to consider the scope of your upgrade and plan for sufficient testing to ensure a seamless transition. Take this guide as a blueprint, adapt it to the specific needs of your project, and always prioritize careful testing for every upgrade process.

Official Upgrade Guidance

Did you know Angular provides official upgrade guidance? If you haven't visited the site, check out the Angular Upgrade Guide or visit the raw URL: `https://update.angular.io/`

My Project

The application I'll be upgrading is the showcase project from my book and course on Ionic and Angular development. This is an Ionic application, developed with a responsive design to function smoothly on both desktop and mobile platforms.

Previously, I had updated the application to Angular 12 and then paused its development for a period. Now, with Angular 16 being the current version (as of the time of writing), I want to further update the application to leverage Angular's latest features.

For a glimpse of the application before the upgrade process, you can visit its public GitHub repository at this link: `https://github.com/walkingriver/at10dance-angular`.

In order to keep the application in sync with Angular's evolving capabilities, I've resolved to upgrade it to Angular 16. This ensures that the application continues to operate efficiently, making the most of Angular's cutting-edge features.

Angular 12.x to 12.y

The first thing I did was ensure the project was on the latest version of Angular 12.

It's essential to note that the Angular CLI, during the update process, expects to work on a clean repository, meaning that there should be no uncommitted changes in your project. The reason behind this is simple: should something go awry during the upgrade, it's far easier to revert to a clean state if all of your changes have been committed.

Another critical point is to ensure that all your npm packages are installed before you initiate the upgrade. The Angular CLI inspects your node modules to identify what needs to be updated. If you don't have all your packages installed, it won't have a clear picture of the updates necessary. This could potentially lead to incomplete updates or version mismatches, which could cause errors down the line.

In essence, a clean, up-to-date repository is a prerequisite to a successful, painless upgrade. Prior to launching any upgrade, always ensure your codebase is fully committed and your npm packages are correctly installed.

After confirming a clean repo, I ran the following command:

```
ng update @angular/cli@12 @angular/core@12
```

The command is asking the Angular CLI to update both the Angular CLI package and the Angular core package to version 12 in your project.

This is a common first step in the Angular update process, as you would typically want to ensure your CLI and core framework are aligned in terms of versioning, before moving onto other dependencies in your project.

```
The installed local Angular CLI version is older than the
latest stable version.
Installing a temporary version to perform the update.
✓ Package successfully installed.
Workspace extension with invalid name (defaultProject) found.
Using package manager: npm
Collecting installed dependencies...
Found 42 dependencies.
Fetching dependency metadata from registry...
    Updating package.json with dependency @angular-devkit/
    build-angular @ "12.2.18" (was "12.2.13")...
    Updating package.json with dependency @angular/cli @
    "12.2.18" (was "12.2.13")...
    Updating package.json with dependency @angular/compiler @
    "12.2.17" (was "12.2.13")...
    Updating package.json with dependency @angular/compiler-cli
    @ "12.2.17" (was "12.2.13")...
    Updating package.json with dependency @angular/language-
    service @ "12.2.17" (was "12.2.13")...
    Updating package.json with dependency @angular/common @
    "12.2.17" (was "12.2.13")...
    Updating package.json with dependency @angular/core @
    "12.2.17" (was "12.2.13")...
    Updating package.json with dependency @angular/forms @
    "12.2.17" (was "12.2.13")...
```

```
Updating package.json with dependency @angular/platform-
browser @ "12.2.17" (was "12.2.13")...
Updating package.json with dependency @angular/platform-
browser-dynamic @ "12.2.17" (was "12.2.13")...
Updating package.json with dependency @angular/router @
"12.2.17" (was "12.2.13")...
Updating package.json with dependency typescript @ "4.3.5"
(was "4.3.3")...
```
UPDATE package.json (1841 bytes)

✓ Packages successfully installed.

I specifically instructed the CLI to update to @angular/cli and @angular/core version 12, which will upgrade to the latest minor/revision of that major version.

Next, I committed the changes. As I said, Angular will not update on an unclean working repo.

```
git commit -am "Updated Angular to latest 12.x"
```

Not much happened because it was such a minor upgrade. The Angular schematics didn't detect any code changes required, which will not always be the case, as I'm sure we'll see. At this point, and after each upgrade, it is a good idea to test your application to ensure everything is working as expected. If you have automated tests, this step will be much easier.

Angular 12 to Angular 13

A significant transition occurs when upgrading from Angular 12 to Angular 13. This is the point where Ivy, Angular's latest rendering pipeline and view engine, becomes mandatory. Ivy was introduced as the default rendering engine with Angular 9, providing improvements in bundle size, debugging, build times, and type checking. While it was optional from version 9 to 12, giving developers ample time to transition, it was not until Angular 13 that the older View Engine was fully retired.

As such, when you make the leap from Angular 12 to 13, you are also making a commitment to Ivy. It is crucial to understand that after Angular 12, there is no going back to the View Engine. This switch carries both opportunities and responsibilities. You gain access to the advancements that Ivy brings, but you also take on the task of ensuring your codebase is compatible with this new engine.

Upgrading to Angular 13 implies embracing Ivy wholeheartedly, and as such, you should test your application thoroughly to ensure that it behaves as expected with the new rendering engine.

Upgrading the Project to Angular 13

I upgraded the project to Angular 13 with the following command:

```
ng update @angular/cli@13 @angular/core@13
```

At this point I ran into my first snag. There were errors during the package installation phase of the update.

```
The installed Angular CLI version is outdated.
Installing a temporary Angular CLI versioned 13.3.11 to perform
the update.
✓ Package successfully installed.
Using package manager: 'npm'
Collecting installed dependencies...
Found 42 dependencies.
Fetching dependency metadata from registry...
Updating package.json with dependency @angular-devkit/build-
angular @ "13.3.11" (was "12.2.18")...
Updating package.json with dependency @angular/cli @ "13.3.11"
(was "12.2.18")...
```

Updating package.json with dependency @angular/compiler @ "13.4.0" (was "12.2.17")...
Updating package.json with dependency @angular/compiler-cli @ "13.4.0" (was "12.2.17")...
Updating package.json with dependency @angular/language-service @ "13.4.0" (was "12.2.17")...
Updating package.json with dependency typescript @ "4.6.4" (was "4.3.5")...
Updating package.json with dependency @angular/common @ "13.4.0" (was "12.2.17")...
Updating package.json with dependency @angular/core @ "13.4.0" (was "12.2.17")...
Updating package.json with dependency @angular/forms @ "13.4.0" (was "12.2.17")...
Updating package.json with dependency @angular/platform-browser @ "13.4.0" (was "12.2.17")...
Updating package.json with dependency @angular/platform-browser-dynamic @ "13.4.0" (was "12.2.17")...
Updating package.json with dependency @angular/router @ "13.4.0" (was "12.2.17")...
UPDATE package.json (1832 bytes)
npm ERR! code ERESOLVE
npm ERR! ERESOLVE could not resolve
npm ERR!
npm ERR! While resolving: at10dance@0.0.1
npm ERR! Found: @angular-devkit/build-angular@12.2.18
npm ERR! node_modules/@angular-devkit/build-angular
npm ERR! dev @angular-devkit/build-angular@"~13.3.11" from the root project
npm ERR! peer @angular-devkit/build-angular@">=0.800.0" from @ionic/angular-toolkit@2.2.0

```
npm ERR! node_modules/@ionic/angular-toolkit
npm ERR! dev @ionic/angular-toolkit@"^2.1.1" from the
root project
npm ERR!
npm ERR! Could not resolve dependency:
npm ERR! dev @angular-devkit/build-angular@"~13.3.11" from the
root project
npm ERR!
npm ERR! Conflicting peer dependency: @angular/compiler-
cli@13.4.0
npm ERR! node_modules/@angular/compiler-cli
npm ERR! peer @angular/compiler-cli@"^13.0.0 || ^13.3.0-rc.0"
from @angular-devkit/build-angular@13.3.11
npm ERR! node_modules/@angular-devkit/build-angular
npm ERR! dev @angular-devkit/build-angular@"~13.3.11" from the
root project
npm ERR!
npm ERR! Fix the upstream dependency conflict, or retry
npm ERR! this command with --force or --legacy-peer-deps
npm ERR! to accept an incorrect (and potentially broken)
dependency resolution.
```

Let's unpack that and see what we can do about it. It appears that there are some dependency problems. At this point, I cannot even run a simple npm install without encountering these errors.

I temporarily sidestepped the errors by using npm install --legacy-peer-deps. The --legacy-peer-deps flag is a feature of npm that reverts to the old peer dependencies algorithm from npm version 6. In npm v7, the handling of peer dependencies was changed to automatically install them (whereas in npm v6 and earlier, they were not installed by default). This means that, in npm v7, if there are incompatible peer dependencies, the installation will fail.

The `--legacy-peer-deps` command circumvents this by ignoring peer dependencies, allowing the install process to continue even if there are incompatible versions. This flag can be handy as a temporary solution when you're trying to resolve conflicts, but it's not a long-term fix.

Why did it work? Essentially, this command worked because it bypassed the stricter peer dependency resolutions that npm 7 employs and reverted to the npm 6 way of handling things. This means it did not halt the install process due to incompatible peer dependencies.

However, it's important to note that using this flag as a long-term solution is not advisable. It essentially silences the errors and warnings, which are there for a reason: to help maintain the compatibility and stability of your project. Ignoring peer dependencies could lead to unpredictable behavior, subtle bugs, or even outright application crashes if the dependencies rely on certain features or behaviors of each other.

In general, it's best to address the root cause of the conflict. This could involve updating packages to versions that are compatible with each other, seeking alternatives to certain packages, or reaching out to package maintainers to address compatibility issues. Always consider the `--legacy-peer-deps` option as a last resort, and even then, only for short-term fixes.

Upgrading Ionic and Other Dependencies

It appears I have some older versions of Ionic and Capacitor that also need to be addressed. Though I had intended to ignore those for this text, upgrading other critical dependencies is definitely a scenario that should be addressed, so I'll do that now. My guess is that once these dependencies are updated, many of the other dependency issues will be resolved also.

Fortunately, Ionic can be updated with the Angular CLI. I know that Ionic is on version 7, but I'll hold off until Angular is updated to 16.

```
ng update @ionic/angular@6
```

At this point, my confidence level wasn't high. You may be experiencing that yourself, wondering how bad your project will be to update. As you should always do with each major upgrade, I decided to run the app to see how it worked. Fortunately, other than a few typos I noticed, it worked as expected.

Angular 13 to Angular 14

After breathing a sigh of relief, I committed the repo's changes and then let the CLI upgrade from Angular 13 to Angular 14. Hopefully, there won't be any more surprises, but if so, I'll deal with them as they arise.

```
ng update @angular/cli@14 @angular/core@14
```

Thankfully, this command completed without any of the dependency issues. However, as you'll see, this is the first update that required Angular to make changes to my project itself.

```
The installed Angular CLI version is outdated.
Installing a temporary Angular CLI versioned 14.2.12 to perform
the update.
✓ Package successfully installed.
Using package manager: npm
Collecting installed dependencies...
Found 42 dependencies.
Fetching dependency metadata from registry...
Updating package.json with dependency @angular-devkit/build-
angular @ "14.2.12" (was "13.3.11")...
Updating package.json with dependency @angular/cli @ "14.2.12"
(was "13.3.11")...
Updating package.json with dependency @angular/compiler @
"14.3.0" (was "13.4.0")...
```

Updating package.json with dependency @angular/compiler-cli @
"14.3.0" (was "13.4.0")...
Updating package.json with dependency @angular/language-service
@ "14.3.0" (was "13.4.0")...
Updating package.json with dependency @angular/common @
"14.3.0" (was "13.4.0")...
Updating package.json with dependency @angular/core @ "14.3.0"
(was "13.4.0")...
Updating package.json with dependency @angular/forms @ "14.3.0"
(was "13.4.0")...
Updating package.json with dependency @angular/platform-browser
@ "14.3.0" (was "13.4.0")...
Updating package.json with dependency @angular/platform-
browser-dynamic @ "14.3.0" (was "13.4.0")...
Updating package.json with dependency @angular/router @
"14.3.0" (was "13.4.0")...
UPDATE package.json (1824 bytes)
✓ Packages successfully installed.
Executing migrations of package '@angular/cli'
〉 Remove 'defaultProject' option from workspace configuration.
   The project to use will be determined from the current
   working directory.
UPDATE angular.json (5630 bytes)
   Migration completed.
〉 Remove 'showCircularDependencies' option from browser and
server builders.
   Migration completed.
〉 Replace 'defaultCollection' option in workspace configuration
with 'schematicCollections'.
UPDATE angular.json (5647 bytes)
   Migration completed.

> Update Angular packages 'dependencies' and 'devDependencies' version prefix to '^' instead of '~'.
UPDATE package.json (1824 bytes)
✓ Packages installed successfully.
  Migration completed.
> Remove 'package.json' files from library projects secondary entrypoints.
  Migration completed.
> Update TypeScript compilation target to 'ES2020'.
UPDATE tsconfig.json (516 bytes)
  Migration completed.
Executing migrations of package '@angular/core'
> As of Angular version 13, `entryComponents` are no longer necessary.
UPDATE src/app/app.module.ts (584 bytes)
  Migration completed.
> In Angular version 14, the `pathMatch` property of `Routes` was updated to be a strict union of the two valid options: `'full'|'prefix'`.
  `Routes` and `Route` variables need an explicit type so
    TypeScript does not infer the property as the looser `string`.
  Migration completed.
> As of Angular version 14, Forms model classes accept a type parameter, and existing usages must be opted out to preserve backwards-compatibility.
  Migration completed.

Most of these were informational. You can read the messages for yourself, but there are a few things I want to point out:

- Changed the target in tsconfig.json from es2015 to es2020: The target option in the tsconfig.json file tells the TypeScript compiler which version of ECMAScript (the standard that defines JavaScript) to use when transpiling your TypeScript code into JavaScript. By changing the target from es2015 to es2020, Angular is updating your project to use more modern JavaScript features that are part of the ECMAScript 2020 specification. This can include features like optional chaining, nullish coalescing, and more. This is consistent with Angular dropping support for Internet Explorer.

- Removed entryComponents array from app.module. ts: In Angular versions prior to 9, the entryComponents array in the NgModule decorator was used to define components that are not found in HTML templates (i.e., components that are dynamically loaded). With the introduction of the Ivy compiler in Angular 9, this array is no longer necessary because Ivy can compile and cache these components as needed, so Angular removes it during the update process.

- Added "defaultProject": "app" to angular.json: The defaultProject option in the angular.json file specifies which project should be built, served, etc., when no project name is provided in the CLI command. By setting "defaultProject": "app", Angular is specifying that the app project should be the default. This is particularly useful in workspaces with multiple projects, as it allows you to run commands like ng serve or ng build without specifying a project name.

As before, I double-checked that the application was still functional. Then, I committed the code and checked the behavior of the application.

Angular 14 to Angular 15

Next, I upgraded from Angular 14 to Angular 15.

```
ng update @angular/cli@15 @angular/core@15
```

```
The installed Angular CLI version is outdated. Installing a
temporary Angular CLI versioned 15.2.9 to perform the update.
✓ Packages successfully installed.
Using package manager: npm
Collecting installed dependencies...
Found 42 dependencies.
Fetching dependency metadata from registry...
    Updating package.json with dependency @angular-devkit/
    build-angular @ "15.2.9" (was "14.2.12")...
    Updating package.json with dependency @angular/cli @
    "15.2.9" (was "14.2.12")...
    Updating package.json with dependency @angular/compiler @
    "15.2.9" (was "14.3.0")...
    Updating package.json with dependency @angular/compiler-cli
    @ "15.2.9" (was "14.3.0")...
    Updating package.json with dependency @angular/language-
    service @ "15.2.9" (was "14.3.0")...
    Updating package.json with dependency typescript @ "4.9.5"
    (was "4.6.4")...
    Updating package.json with dependency @angular/common @
    "15.2.9" (was "14.3.0")...
    Updating package.json with dependency @angular/core @
    "15.2.9" (was "14.3.0")...
```

Updating package.json with dependency @angular/forms @ "15.2.9" (was "14.3.0")...
Updating package.json with dependency @angular/platform-browser @ "15.2.9" (was "14.3.0")...
Updating package.json with dependency @angular/platform-browser-dynamic @ "15.2.9" (was "14.3.0")...
Updating package.json with dependency @angular/router @ "15.2.9" (was "14.3.0")...
UPDATE package.json (1822 bytes)
✓ Packages successfully installed.
** Executing migrations of package '@angular/cli' **
⟩ Remove Browserslist configuration files that matches the Angular CLI default configuration.
  Migration completed (No changes made).
⟩ Remove exported `@angular/platform-server` `renderModule` method.
  The `renderModule` method is now exported by the Angular CLI.
  Migration completed (No changes made).
⟩ Remove no longer needed require calls in Karma builder main file.
UPDATE src/test.ts (459 bytes)
  Migration completed (1 file modified).
⟩ Update TypeScript compiler `target` and set `useDefineForClassFields`.
  These changes are for IDE purposes as TypeScript compiler options `target` and `useDefineForClassFields` are set to `ES2022` and `false` respectively by the Angular CLI.
  To control ECMA version and features use the Browerslist configuration.
UPDATE tsconfig.json (584 bytes)
  Migration completed (1 file modified).

> Remove options from 'angular.json' that are no longer
supported by the official builders.
  Migration completed **(**No changes made**)**.
** Executing migrations of package '@angular/core' **
> In Angular version 15, the deprecated
`relativeLinkResolution` config parameter of the Router is
removed.
  This migration removes all `relativeLinkResolution` fields
  from the Router config objects.
UPDATE src/app/app-routing.module.ts **(**788 bytes**)**
  Migration completed **(**1 file modified**)**.
> Since Angular v15, the `RouterLink` contains the logic of the
`RouterLinkWithHref` directive.
  This migration replaces all `RouterLinkWithHref` references
  with `RouterLink`.
  Migration completed **(**No changes made**)**.

That was a lot, but reviewing the changes, it didn't do much. One thing worth pointing out is a change it made to tsconfig.json. It added "useDefineForClassFields": false to the end of the compilerOptions section.

The "useDefineForClassFields": false setting in TypeScript ensures that class fields are initialized after the constructor is called. This is important for Angular components that use dependency injection in the constructor and initialize class fields with values that depend on these injected dependencies.

For example, consider an Angular component that uses a value from the ActivatedRoute service to initialize a class field:

```
@Component({
  selector: "my-component",
  template: `{{ name }}`,
})
```

```
export class MyComponent {
  name = this.getName();

  constructor(private route: ActivatedRoute) {}

  getName(): string {
    return this.route.snapshot.paramMap.get("name");
  }
}
```

With "useDefineForClassFields": true, TypeScript would try to initialize name before route is defined, causing an error. By setting "useDefineForClassFields": false, TypeScript initializes name after the constructor is called, ensuring route is defined when getName is called.

Had the Angular team not made this decision, many existing Angular apps would break when upgraded to Angular 15 and its updated version of TypeScript.

After that, I once again reviewed the application's behavior. When I was satisfied, I committed the code and moved on.

Angular 15 to Angular 16

Finally, I asked the CLI to upgrade from Angular 15 to Angular 16.

```
ng update @angular/cli@16 @angular/core@16
The installed Angular CLI version is outdated.
Installing a temporary Angular CLI versioned 16.1.4 to perform
the update.
✓ Packages successfully installed.
Using package manager: npm
Collecting installed dependencies...
Found 42 dependencies.
Fetching dependency metadata from registry...
```

Updating package.json with dependency @angular-devkit/build-angular @ "16.1.4" (was "15.2.9")...
Updating package.json with dependency @angular/cli @ "16.1.4" (was "15.2.9")...
Updating package.json with dependency @angular/compiler @ "16.1.5" (was "15.2.9")...
Updating package.json with dependency @angular/compiler-cli @ "16.1.5" (was "15.2.9")...
Updating package.json with dependency @angular/language-service @ "16.1.5" (was "15.2.9")...
Updating package.json with dependency @angular/common @ "16.1.5" (was "15.2.9")...
Updating package.json with dependency @angular/core @ "16.1.5" (was "15.2.9")...
Updating package.json with dependency @angular/forms @ "16.1.5" (was "15.2.9")...
Updating package.json with dependency @angular/platform-browser @ "16.1.5" (was "15.2.9")...
Updating package.json with dependency @angular/platform-browser-dynamic @ "16.1.5" (was "15.2.9")...
Updating package.json with dependency @angular/router @ "16.1.5" (was "15.2.9")...
Updating package.json with dependency zone.js @ "0.13.1" (was "0.11.4")...
UPDATE package.json (1822 bytes)
✓ Packages successfully installed.

Executing migrations of package '@angular/cli':
> Remove 'defaultProject' option from workspace configuration.
  The project to use will be determined from the current
  working directory.
  Migration completed (No changes made).

> Replace removed 'defaultCollection' option in workspace
configuration with 'schematicCollections'.
  Migration completed (No changes made).

> Update the '@angular-devkit/build-angular:server'
builder configuration to disable 'buildOptimizer' for non
optimized builds.
  Migration completed (No changes made).

Executing migrations of package '@angular/core':
> In Angular version 15.2, the guard and resolver interfaces
(CanActivate, Resolve, etc) were deprecated.
  This migration removes imports and 'implements' clauses that
  contain them.
  Migration completed (No changes made).
> As of Angular v16, the `moduleId` property of `@Component` is
deprecated as it no longer has any effect.
  Migration completed (No changes made).

It didn't make any code or configuration changes to my project,
which is understandable. While Angular 16 added a lot of functionality, it
didn't remove or change anything major. However, I do want to point out
one very important thing that will be an issue in the next release or two.
Specifically, this message:

> In Angular version 15.2, the guard and resolver interfaces
(CanActivate, Resolve, etc) were deprecated.

The shift from class-based to functional interfaces for guards and
resolvers in Angular is part of a broader industry trend towards functional
programming, which offers several advantages:

- Testability: Functional code is generally easier to test
  because it doesn't rely on external state. Each function
  is self-contained, taking inputs and producing outputs
  without side effects.

- Simplicity: Functional interfaces are typically simpler and more straightforward than class-based interfaces. They don't require the new keyword to create an instance and don't have the this context, which can be a source of confusion.

- Tree-shaking: Functional code is more amenable to tree-shaking, a process used by modern bundlers to eliminate unused code and reduce the size of the final bundle. This can lead to smaller, faster applications.

In the context of Angular, the shift to functional interfaces for guards and resolvers means that you can now use simple functions instead of classes to define your guards and resolvers. This can make your code cleaner, easier to understand, and potentially more efficient.

However, it's important to note that while the class-based interfaces are deprecated, they will continue to work for some time to ensure backward compatibility. You should plan to migrate to the new functional interfaces at your earliest convenience to take advantage of their benefits and stay up-to-date with Angular's evolution.

I'll talk more about that in a later chapter.

A Note on the Angular CLI

You may have noticed that each Angular update started with a message about the installed CLI being outdated. My globally installed version is 16.1.4, which is the latest version available at this time. The message displayed during the update process was because the Angular CLI detected a version mismatch between the currently installed CLI and the targeted version of Angular. Ultimately, it doesn't really matter. The Angular CLI and ng update will do the right thing.

Summary

In this chapter, we explored the importance of regularly updating your Angular projects, the benefits it brings, as well as the potential pitfalls if neglected.

Regularly updating your Angular projects is critical for a number of reasons:

- Security: Outdated versions can have unresolved security vulnerabilities, leaving your application open to potential threats.

- Support: As of this writing, Angular versions 12 and older are already unsupported. This means if your application is on an unsupported version, you may face challenges getting help with bugs or issues.

- Access to New Features: Each new version of Angular brings a host of improvements, enhancements, and new features that can make your development process smoother and your application more efficient and performant.

- Performance Enhancements: Newer versions of Angular often come with optimizations and performance enhancements, which can improve the overall performance and user experience of your applications.

However, there are potential pitfalls if you let your project fall too far behind:

- Complex upgrade process: Upgrading across multiple major versions at once can become complex and time-consuming, often requiring extensive testing and debugging.

- Deprecated features: Older versions may rely on features or APIs that are deprecated in newer versions. When these are removed, it can cause breaking changes in your application.

- Package compatibility issues: Newer Angular versions may have incompatibilities with older versions of certain packages, which can lead to version conflicts and can make the update process complicated.

By regularly updating your Angular applications – ideally staying current or no more than n-2 versions behind – you can mitigate these challenges. Angular's iterative approach to updates, with few breaking changes from release to release, makes this a manageable task. With strategic version control and frequent testing, you can take advantage of the latest Angular offerings while keeping your projects secure and performant.

As you navigate the update process, remember to always have a clean repository, ensure your npm packages are installed, and have a compatible version of Angular CLI. While there are workarounds to package conflicts, like the `npm install --legacy-peer-deps` command, these are not long-term solutions and it's crucial to resolve these issues promptly.

Finally, using appropriate versions of associated technologies, like I did with Ionic, that are compatible with your Angular version ensures smoother functioning of your application. It's always recommended to refer to the official documentation to keep abreast with these specifications.

Keeping your Angular projects updated is an essential part of maintaining a secure, efficient, and highly performant application that can continue to grow and evolve with the ever-changing web development landscape.

While your upgrade experience might differ from mine, I hope the information has been helpful. Wishing you every success in your own endeavors.

CHAPTER 9

Standalone Components

Introduced as a developer preview in Angular 15.2, standalone components in Angular mark a significant step towards simplifying the development process. They eliminate the need for `NgModules`, streamlining the developer experience and making the code more concise and clear. This new approach allows developers to specify dependencies directly within components, without having to navigate through `NgModules`.

SCAM Pattern

Prior to standalone components, many Angular developers turned to a pattern that became known as SCAM. The SCAM pattern in Angular stands for Single Component Angular Module. It's a design pattern where each Angular component is paired with its own Angular module.

The SCAM pattern emerged as a response to some of the complexities and challenges associated with traditional Angular module organization. In a typical Angular application, components, directives, and pipes are often grouped into shared or feature modules. While this approach has its advantages, it can lead to challenges in understanding dependencies, promoting reusability, and optimizing performance.

M. D. Callaghan, *Angular for Business*, https://doi.org/10.1007/978-1-4842-9609-7_9

The SCAM pattern addresses these challenges by providing a clear and concise way to organize components and their dependencies. It aligns with modern development practices and the trend towards more modular and maintainable code.

Introduction to Standalone Components

Standalone Components in Angular are a more recent development that aims to simplify the structure of Angular applications by reducing the reliance on NgModules. While the SCAM pattern provided a way to encapsulate components with their dependencies, Standalone Components take this concept further by eliminating the need for additional modules altogether.

Another thing that makes standalone components particularly appealing is their ability to be adopted incrementally. Existing applications can embrace this new style without any breaking changes, providing a smooth transition path. Moreover, standalone components are compatible with existing `NgModule`-based libraries and dependencies, allowing developers to take full advantage of the existing Angular ecosystem.

The introduction of standalone components also brings enhancements to routing and lazy loading. The updated router APIs are designed to work seamlessly with standalone components, simplifying common lazy-loading scenarios and removing the need for an `NgModule`. This not only makes the code cleaner but also enhances the application's performance.

Eliminates app.module.ts

Bootstrapping an Angular application has also become more straightforward with standalone components. Developers can now bootstrap without any `NgModule`, using a standalone component as the root. This further simplifies the application structure and reduces boilerplate code.

Library authors will find standalone components beneficial as well. They can export standalone components, directives, and pipes, offering more flexibility in structuring and distributing their libraries. This pattern is useful for creating sets of cooperating directives that work together to form a logical unit, such as a carousel widget.

Standalone components also introduce new ways of configuring dependency injection. The concept of environment injectors and standalone injectors provides more control and flexibility over how dependencies are managed. This new configuration pattern supports more advanced usage patterns and ensures that standalone components are truly self-contained, preventing any "leakage" of implementation details into the rest of the application.

Upgrading Your Angular App to Standalone

If you want to migrate your NgModule-based app to Standalone, the Angular CLI provides a migration schematic to do most of the work for you, which I will demonstrate here. It's not foolproof, as we'll soon see.

I will continue the application upgrade from the prior chapter by migrating the entire app to standalone components. I'll show the steps, but only some of the resulting code, where it helps to illustrate what's going on.

Preparing for Migration

If you want to follow along with your own app, ensure that your project is using Angular 15.2.0 or later. I just upgraded mine to 16 in the last chapter, so I've got that covered. Make sure the project builds without any compilation errors and that you have no uncommitted changes. It also helps to start with a clean branch, which I'll do here to save all my work.

```
> git checkout -b standalone-migration
Switched to a new branch 'standalone-migration'
```

Running the Schematic

I initiated the migration by running the following command, which offered a few options. This is a multi-step process, and I'll show each step and some of what changed. I selected the first option to convert all components, directives, and pipes to standalone.

```
> ng generate @angular/core:standalone

? Choose the type of migration: (Use arrow keys)
> Convert all components, directives and pipes to standalone
  Remove unnecessary NgModule classes
  Bootstrap the application using standalone APIs
? Which path in your project should be migrated? (./)
```

```
  🎉 Automated migration step has finished! 🎉
  IMPORTANT! Please verify manually that your application
  builds and behaves as expected.
  See https://angular.io/guide/standalone-migration for more
  information.
UPDATE src/app/home/home.page.ts (402 bytes)
UPDATE src/app/student-info/student-info.page.ts (2390 bytes)
UPDATE src/app/roster/roster.page.ts (3071 bytes)
UPDATE src/app/home/home.module.ts (423 bytes)
UPDATE src/app/student-info/student-info.module.ts (521 bytes)
UPDATE src/app/roster/roster.module.ts (437 bytes)
UPDATE src/app/app.component.spec.ts (2218 bytes)
UPDATE src/app/home/home.page.spec.ts (636 bytes)
UPDATE src/app/roster/roster.page.spec.ts (650 bytes)
UPDATE src/app/student-info/student-info.page.spec.ts
(686 bytes)
```

Review a Change

Let's take a look at one of the Angular components to see what the migration scripts did. I'll show only the semantically meaningful changes to the Roster page component.

Before:

```
@Component({
  selector: 'app-student-info',
  templateUrl: './student-info.page.html',
  styleUrls: ['./student-info.page.scss'],
})
```

After:

```
@Component({
    selector: 'app-student-info',
    templateUrl: './student-info.page.html',
    styleUrls: ['./student-info.page.scss'],
    standalone: true,
    imports: [
        NgIf,
        IonicModule,
        FormsModule,
        AsyncPipe,
        JsonPipe,
    ],
})
```

At first, you may be wondering how adding *more* code is a good thing. Remember that we'll be removing an entire NgModule, so please trust the process for now.

The migration added the `standalone: true` property to the component's metadata, marking it as a standalone component. An `imports` array was also added, listing the dependencies that this component relies on, including the newly imported modules and directives. Standalone components need to tell Angular about other components and modules they plan to use. The tradeoff is that by adding these imports here explicitly, Angular's tree-shaking is able to remove unused components more intelligently, potentially leading to smaller bundle sizes. Some of these would have been imported into the page's ngModule or in app.module.ts, but those will both be deleted soon.

After that, I ran the application and tests to ensure everything was working as expected. I'm probably being over cautious, but I also committed the changes to my Git repository before taking the next step.

Step 2: Remove Unnecessary NgModule Classes

Next, I needed to remove unnecessary NgModule classes. With standalone components, I don't need any of the individual component modules, nor do I need their individual routing modules. However, I do need to make sure that each page's routes are moved to the app-routing module.

Ever the optimist, I tried running the migration script again, this time selecting the second option.

```
> ng generate @angular/core:standalone

? Choose the type of migration:
  Convert all components, directives and pipes to standalone
> Remove unnecessary NgModule classes
  Bootstrap the application using standalone APIs
? Which path in your project should be migrated? ./
  🎉 Automated migration step has finished! 🎉
  IMPORTANT! Please verify manually that your application
  builds and behaves as expected.
```

See https://angular.io/guide/standalone-migration for more
information.
Nothing to be done.

This was unexpected until I thought it about it some. As I said, I tend to
use the SCAM pattern on my Angular apps and this app was no exception.
Apparently, the Angular CLI migration doesn't know how to do that, which
is a little disappointing.

That meant I had to do this manually. As I said before, I needed to
move each page's routing into app-routing.module.ts and then I could
simply delete the modules for each component.

Routing

Let's take a look at the app-routing before and after.

Before:

```
{
  path: 'home',
  loadChildren: () =>
    import('./home/home.module').then((m) => m.HomePageModule),
},
{
  path: 'student-info',
  loadChildren: () =>
    import('./student-info/student-info.module').then(
      (m) => m.StudentInfoPageModule
    ),
},
{
  path: 'roster',
  loadChildren: () =>
```

```
import('./roster/roster.module').then((m) =>
m.RosterPageModule),
```

},

After:

```
{
  path: 'home',
  loadComponent: () => import('./home/home.page').then((m) =>
  m.HomePage),
},
{
  path: 'student-info',
  children: [
    {
      path: ':id',
      loadComponent: () => import('./student-info/student-info.
      page').then((m) => m.StudentInfoPage),
    }
  ]
},
{
  path: 'roster',
  loadComponent: () => import('./roster/roster.page').then((m)
  => m.RosterPage),
},
```

Initially, I was leveraging the loadChildren method to lazily load entire modules. By replacing those with standalone components, that was no longer necessary, or even possible. So, I transitioned to the loadComponent field, which has essentially the same syntax. You import the component directly by file name, which returns a promise. Once it's loaded, you can grab the component itself in a type-safe manager in the callback.

It's a subtle change, but it significantly improved the code's readability, ensuring that future developers can navigate it with ease.

Once I did that, I was able to delete all the existing components' modules and run the app again.

Ionic 6.x Warning

This is a book about Angular, not Ionic. That said, I do want to point out one additional change I needed to make, given that the app in question uses Ionic components.

Ionic 6 supported standalone components through the use of an environment injector. Without that, an Angular app using Ionic with standalone components wouldn't work. The symptom is that the app won't render anything but a white screen.

Conveniently, the fix is printed right in the browser console.

To fix it, you simply add a couple of lines of code.

Before: app.component.ts

```
constructor(private platform: Platform, private students:
StudentsService) {
  this.initializeApp();
}
```

After: app.component.ts

```
constructor(public environmentInjector: EnvironmentInjector,
private platform: Platform, private students: StudentsService) {
  this.initializeApp();
}
```

I added the EnvironmentInjector object into my app component's constructor. Then, in the app component's HTML file, I used Angular data binding to insert it into the `<ion-router-outlet>`.

Before: app.component.html

```
<ion-router-outlet id="main-content"></ion-router-outlet>
```

After: app.component.html

```
<ion-router-outlet id="main-content" [environmentInjector]="environmentInjector"></ion-router-outlet>
```

Note   Ionic 7 solves this problem entirely by supporting standalone components natively.

Step 3: Bootstrap the Project Using Standalone APIs

As the final step, I bootstrapped the project using standalone APIs. That meant running the schematic one last time.

```
> npx ng generate @angular/core:standalone
? Choose the type of migration:
  Convert all components, directives and pipes to standalone
  Remove unnecessary NgModule classes
> Bootstrap the application using standalone APIs
? Which path in your project should be migrated? ./
    📣 Automated migration step has finished! 📣
    IMPORTANT! Please verify manually that your application
    builds and behaves as expected.
```

See https://angular.io/guide/standalone-migration for more information.

DELETE src/app/app.module.ts
UPDATE src/main.ts (995 bytes)
UPDATE src/app/app.component.ts (1159 bytes)
UPDATE src/app/app.component.spec.ts (2198 bytes)

Let's review what it did.

Before: app.component.ts

```
@Component({
    selector: 'app-root',
    templateUrl: 'app.component.html',
    styleUrls: ['app.component.scss'],
})
```

After: app.component.ts

```
@Component({
    selector: 'app-root',
    templateUrl: 'app.component.html',
    styleUrls: ['app.component.scss'],
    standalone: true,
    imports: [
        IonicModule,
        NgFor,
        RouterLinkActive,
        RouterLink,
    ],
})
```

In the `app.component.ts`, the schematic added the `standalone: true` property to the `@Component` decorator. Moreover, the necessary dependencies like `IonicModule`, `NgFor`, `RouterLinkActive`, and `RouterLink` were moved directly into the component's `imports` array.

The schematic then deleted the `app.module.ts` file completely.

Before: main.ts

```
platformBrowserDynamic()
  .bootstrapModule(AppModule)
  .catch((err) => console.log(err));
```

After: main.ts

```
bootstrapApplication(AppComponent, {
  providers: [importProvidersFrom(BrowserModule, IonicModule.
  forRoot(), AppRoutingModule), { provide: RouteReuseStrategy,
  useClass: IonicRouteStrategy }],
}).catch((err) => console.log(err));
```

In `main.ts`, rather than using the conventional `bootstrapModule` method to start the application with a module, the schematic changed it to call the `bootstrapApplication` function to initiate the app directly. Required providers and configurations were directly imported and integrated during this bootstrapping phase.

Does It Work?

Automatic upgrade code is great, but to be useful, it still has to work properly. I fired up the app with `npm start` and quickly ran through its functionality. It all worked as expected.

Satisfied with the results of the migration, I committed the code and pushed to my repository on GitHub.

Summary

Migrating to standalone components in Angular was a significant transformation, but by taking a methodical approach, I ensured a successful migration. Regularly committing changes, running tests, and verifying the application's functionality at each stage gave me confidence in the process. I'm pleased with the result, and I feel that my codebase is now more streamlined and maintainable, aligning with modern development practices.

CHAPTER 10

Understand Your Service API

Whether you are creating or consuming an API, you must understand all its implications. If you are the consumer, it is up to you to understand what calling its various functions will do. If you are creating an API, you also have a responsibility to your consumers. I will not go into all the rules here but will touch on two very severe problems that I have personally experienced in my professional life.

Consumer: Know Your API Behavior

This story is a few years old. It is an amusing tale, though it could have been tragic had the code gotten deployed to our production servers.

A few years ago, I was reviewing some .NET code, using LINQ to Entities. I came across a line like the following:

```
var reservations = dataManager.Reservations()
    .ToList()
    .Where(res => res.GuestLastName == lastName);
```

The author's intention in English was the following:

"Get me a list of all reservations where the guest's last name matches the last name provided."

© Michael D. Callaghan 2024
M. D. Callaghan, *Angular for Business*, https://doi.org/10.1007/978-1-4842-9609-7_10

Anyone who has used LINQ to Entities can probably spot the problem immediately. By default, LINQ to Entities executes as much of the query as it can on the database. However, the ToList() call, which is not even necessary, overrides that behavior. It causes the query to be executed immediately and the results serialized into a list. That list is then returned to the method chain, at which point the Where clause is executed.

In English, the actual consequence of this method chain is

"Get me a list of all reservations in the database. Once you've returned all of those to me, then filter the list to only those records with a matching last name provided."

As I am sure you can imagine, asking a hotel reservation system to return all its reservations, without any constraints, would return a lot of records. You might think this would be discovered quickly. The developer did not see any issues locally, because the local development database contained only a few dozen reservations. That is a problem worth its own discussion.

One proper way to write the previous query would be

```
var reservations = dataManager.Reservations()
    .Where(res => res.GuestLastName == lastName);
```

Simply removing the ToList() method causes the entire query to be executed on the database. Only the matching records are returned to the caller. Granted, there are still issues to be addressed, and those issues require an understanding of not only the API, but the database schema.

For example, it probably would not make sense to return all matching records. You may want to limit the number returned to a sizable chunk, and page the rest. It is also possible that the GuestLastName column is not indexed properly, which would result in a table scan of potentially millions of records.

The important thing is that it is up to you, as the API consumer, to know what is really going on. Do not simply and blindly make function calls and hope for the best. You probably do not want to be the one responsible for bringing down your company's production reservations system.

Creators: Do Not Break Your Consumers

This one happened to me recently. A web service I had been using for months now suddenly started returning errors instead of valid search results. I discovered this because I always search for myself when searching in our test environment. I type my last name, and my first initial. This has worked as long as I have been using it.

There are exactly two matching results in our database of hundreds of thousands of people, so it is a convenient search for me to use. This week, however, it started throwing "validation exceptions." Apparently, someone maintaining the web service decided that if you are searching by first and last name, you must include at least two letters for each. I guess that might make sense, to limit the amount of data returned (see above). There are better ways to handle this, though.

They also changed another search, requiring the zip code to be provided. Again, this was done without warning. Quite frankly, if they need to limit the number of records returned, fine. I have one request: tell your API consumers about it ahead of time! Better still, create a new search method updated with the new validation rules or required parameters, deprecate the existing method, and give your consumers ample time to migrate. This will prevent last-minute system outages as your API consumer applications suddenly stop working and cannot figure out why code that worked yesterday suddenly stopped working today.

Summary

If you are consuming an API

- Know how to use the API.

- Understand what the possible replies might be, and ensure that you do not overwhelm any service that might be behind it.

If you are creating an API

- Know how your API is used.

- Build your API to protect yourself; do not return responses that are "too big."

- Do not break the interface to your API.

As I said earlier, you do not want to be the one bringing down the production systems on a Sunday morning.

CHAPTER 11

RxJS: To Use or Not to Use?

During a project a couple of years ago, I was rewriting an AngularJS app to Angular 10. During an early code review, there were some concerns that came up about the heavy use of RxJS. I will attempt to address those concerns in this chapter. Of particular note were the following assertions:

- RxJS is hard to learn/read.
- RxJS is hard to test.

Hard to Learn

Admittedly RxJS has a steep learning curve. That said, it should only take a week or so to become accustomed to using it. Once you understand the basics, the more esoteric operators are mostly a matter of finding them. There is a great website that makes this easier, which is where I found the `fromEvent` and `combineLatest` operators I use in the following (`https://rxjs.dev/operator-decision-tree`).

Hard to Test

Testing Angular is itself often an exercise in frustration. The key is knowing what to test and what not to test, which is the subject of another chapter in this book.

© Michael D. Callaghan 2024
M. D. Callaghan, *Angular for Business*, https://doi.org/10.1007/978-1-4842-9609-7_11

Some people go overboard and try to achieve 100% code coverage. I have found that more than about 80–85% is usually counter-productive. Often, people will write brittle (or worse, useless) tests to try to hit some magical coverage number.

RxJS is no more difficult to test than Angular, assuming you write your code to be testable in the first place. This is not always the case, especially when you try to do too much with it at once. My strategy is to create observables that do one thing that I can explain in a comment. For example:

- Convert input event into stream of search terms.

- Make web service call on selection change.

These sorts of observables are reasonably straightforward to write and test. More importantly, they are also straightforward to read and to modify.

The Code

The code in question includes a custom dropdown with search capability. The idea is that you can bind a very long list of items and either select one or search for one by name. The component fires a custom DOM event, `selected-changed`, to indicate that the user has made a new selection.

The dropdown represents a list of "stores." Whenever a store is selected, the app needs to make a web request to load products associated with that store.

Though it renders and behaves like an HTML `<select>` tag, it does not actually contain a `<select>` element. Fortunately, this turned out to be irrelevant.

The first challenge was to figure out what event was being thrown. The docs showed that I could use `(selected-change)="storeChange($event)`, so I wired it up to see what the event looks like. It seemed to be exactly what I had hoped: a custom DOM event.

The next step was to create an Observable I could subscribe to. I created a component variable I could use to subscribe to the event using Angular's @ViewChild decorator.

```
@ViewChild('storeList') storeListDropdown: ElementRef;
```

That led to this small bit of code:

```
this.storeChanged$ = fromEvent(this.storeListDropdown.
nativeElement, "selected-changed").pipe(
  tap((x) => {
    console.log(x);
  })
);
```

Now I could verify whether or not I could truly subscribe to these custom events. A quick test showed that indeed I could. Hurdle one cleared.

Make the Service Call

Next, I needed to take the newly selected value and use it to make a service call. For various reasons, I cannot show the actual call here, but I think I can show enough to get my point across.

I Only Care About Selections

It is possible for the user to select nothing, at which point I do not want to make a service call. So I added a filter to the observable's pipe to ensure I am only getting selections.

```
this.storeChanged$ = fromEvent<CustomEvent>(this.
storeListDropdown.nativeElement, "selected-changed").pipe(
```

```
  filter((x) => x.detail?.value?.length),
  tap((x) => {
    console.log(x.detail.value[0].value);
  })
);
```

With that I was able to confirm that it only fired when the user selects something. There is another use case to clear the results if the user selects nothing, but that is not currently important.

Making the Web Call

Next up was to make the web service call. I modified the tap function to set a component variable that holds the selection, then added a switchMap to call an Angular service that hides the actual HTTP call. Now it looks like this:

```
this.storeChanged$ = fromEvent<CustomEvent>(this.
storeListDropdown.nativeElement, "selected-changed").pipe(
  filter((x) => x.detail?.value?.length),
  tap((x) => {
    this.selectedStore = x.detail.value[0].value;
  }),
  switchMap((x) => this.getProducts(this.selectedStore))
);
```

I could drop the tap and do both the variable assignment and the service call inside of the switchMap operator. I may eventually do that, but for now I like the way that each step is visually separated.

Implementing a Search Filter

A single "store" in this project could return anywhere from zero to potentially hundreds or thousands of products. Each record is small, so for now, we are keeping the filtering of products entirely client-side. To support that, the UI has a search box. Entering anything in the search box should cause the records to be filtered to those records matching the value entered. This called for another observable, which I will show in its entirety.

```
this.searchFilterChanged$ = fromEvent<InputEvent>(this.
searchBox.nativeElement, "input").pipe(
  // tslint:disable-next-line: no-magic-numbers
  debounceTime(300),
  map((_) => {
    this.searchFilter = this.searchBox.nativeElement.value;
    return this.searchFilter;
  }),
  distinctUntilChanged(),
  startWith("")
);
```

As you can see, I start by creating an observable from the HTML input event. That fires an event for every change to the text box. This stream is then sent through another RxJS pipe to do the following:

- The observable is "debounced" so that any value is delayed by 300ms. This prevents the events from coming in too fast as the user types.

- The distinctUntilChanged operator ensures that only changes to the value are sent. In other words, if the user repeatedly presses the space bar and the backspace key in rapid succession, resulting in no change to the text box, my code will never see it. It is unlikely, but possible.

- Inside of map, I assign the value of the <input> element
  to a component variable named searchFilter and
  return that value. This successfully converts the event
  into a string I can use as a search value later.

- The final operator is startWith(''), which will be
  important later. This initializes the observable stream
  with an empty string value.

Pager Component

My final component is another custom one that handles paging. As I said,
the results of the web service can potentially contain thousands of records,
so I want to provide a user a simple way of paging through those results.
Like my other custom component, it also fires a CustomEvent called nav-
selected. I again used fromEvent and set it up similarly to the first one.

```
this.pagerChanged$ = fromEvent<CustomEvent>(this.pager.
nativeElement, "nav-selected").pipe(
  map((x) => x.detail.currentPage),
  startWith(1)
);
```

This is the simplest of the bunch. Inside its pipe, I map the details from
the custom event into the page the user selected. Once again, I start the
stream with a default value.

Combine Them All

Why did I go through all of this instead of simply using Angular event
binding? This is why.

Now that each event is its own individual stream of events, they can easily be combined using the RxJS operator combineLatest. This operator accepts an array of observables as its input and returns a single observable. As its name implies, this observable fires when any of its input observable values changes. Whenever that happens, the subscriber gets the latest value of each of its constituent observables.

The caveat for this operator is that it will not emit an event until each observable in its input array has fired at least once. This is why each of my earlier observables (except the first one) used startWith to set an initial value. The store dropdown did not need one because until the user selects a store, there is no reason to do anything.

How does this all work in practice? Every time the user selects a new store, changes the search filter, or selects a new page on the pager, my subscriber gets the most recent value of each of those three observables. Here is the code.

```
this.filteredProducts$ = combineLatest([this.
storeChanged$, this.searchFilterChanged$, this.
pagerChanged$]).pipe(map(([products, search, page]) => this.
filterProducts(products, search, page)));
```

Inside of the map operator, you can see that each value from the array of observables is passed into its arrow function. I pass those values into a pure function on my component called filterProducts. This function handles the filter and paging on the products array to return a new array of products.

Keep in mind that the return of combineLatest, which is assigned to this.filteredProducts$, is itself an observable. This is important because of what happens next.

Inside the Template

Because of the composition of these three independent observables into a single observable, binding to its results is almost trivial. Inside my HTML template, I have the following markup inside an HTML `<table>` tag.

```
<tr *ngFor="let product of filteredProducts$ | async">
  ...
</tr>
```

By using Angular's `async` pipe, I never need to subscribe or unsubscribe to the observable. Angular handles all that for me. Whenever any of the three source observables changes, the table will update to reflect those changes.

The Benefit of This Approach

I started down this path of using RxJS for user events because I wanted to isolate each event and hide the irrelevant details from its consumers. By using `fromEvent` I am able to tweak and modify each event to get exactly the behavior I am looking for, separate from the others.

With that, the final observable created with `combineLatest` requires no additional manipulation. I can pass the values to a pure function to get exactly the data to be displayed, and then bind that data with a simple `*ngFor` and `async` pipe.

Testing each observable stream independently from the others also becomes almost trivial.

What I really like most about this approach, though, is how extensible it is. When I first wrote this code, I only had the custom dropdown and the text input box for searching. It was all working properly when I decided to add the custom pager control. The result was that I was able to include the pager, set up and test its custom event, and then simply wire it up to the `combineLatest` operator by adding it to the input array. Then I added it as an input to my `filterProducts` function.

What Do Others Think?

I double-checked my philosophy with some people I consider experts, both inside and outside of the team. Here are some of the responses I received (mostly paraphrased):

- "That code is awesome!"

- "For me it's a tradeoff between simplicity (Angular's event bindings) and power (RxJS fromEvent). In the majority of cases, I only need the simple event bindings. As soon as you try doing something special (debounce, filter, delay, etc.), use RxJS."

- "Observables are a heavy pill to swallow. If you get why you'd use it (sync/async feel the same, pure function pipelines of data, deterministic, easier to unit test), cool. Otherwise, hide in the Model layer so dev can play away from 'em elsewhere."

- "I struggled for a long time to understand RxJs (still don't get everything) but once I had a use case, it was a no-brainer to use the library."

- "Every time I have to touch rxjs code it's a major PITA and source of bugs for me. I'm not intelligent enough to understand it, no matter how many rxjs tutorials I read."

Interestingly, some suggested that learning to use state management with NgRx might result in a lower learning curve than raw RxJS. My experience has been the opposite.

Ultimately, I recommend that you use the best tool for the job. If that means going a little outside of your comfort zone to learn RxJS, so be it.

Everything you have seen earlier took about three days start-to-finish to get right, including the unit tests I have not shown. When I began, I knew almost nothing about any of these RxJS operators I ended up using.

Summary

In this chapter, we've explored the key considerations for using RxJS in Angular projects.

While RxJS has a steep learning curve, it's manageable with about a week of focused study. I've also recommended a "Decision Tree" to help you navigate through its operators.

Testing in Angular can be complex, but adding RxJS to the mix doesn't necessarily complicate it further. The key is to write testable code and aim for meaningful code coverage, rather than striving for 100% code coverage.

We've gone through concrete examples that demonstrate how to work with RxJS effectively. This includes creating a custom dropdown, managing selections, making web service calls, and implementing a search filter.

The highlight of the chapter is the use of the `combineLatest` operator to consolidate multiple observables, making your code more maintainable and efficient.

Best Practices for Handling Changes to Input Properties in Angular

The Pros and Cons of Property Setters vs. ngOnChanges

As Angular developers, one of the challenges we often face is how to handle changes to input properties in our components. There are a few different approaches we can take, and in this chapter, we'll take a look at the pros and cons of using property setters versus the ngOnChanges lifecycle hook. We'll also provide some guidelines for deciding which approach is best for your project.

A recent tweet about @Input() changes in Angular got a lot of discussion going. It got enough attention and discussion that I thought it would be valuable to capture the ideas and suggestions into a single place. At the time of this writing, I still haven't decided which of the various approaches I personally prefer, though I will tell you what I did in this particular application.

© Michael D. Callaghan 2024

M. D. Callaghan, *Angular for Business*, https://doi.org/10.1007/978-1-4842-9609-7_12

The Scenario That Started It All

I have a UI component I've written in Angular that needs to display a collection of buttons. The component doesn't know or care what the buttons contain. It simply ensures that only one button is selected at a time and emits an event when that selection changes.

For simplicity, here is one possible use of this component. Think of them as "radio buttons" implemented as a collection of "pill buttons" as you can see in Figure 12-1.

Figure 12-1. *Radio "pill" buttons*

What I want to point out are the captions above each button. When I started to implement this component, I found an existing component in my project that implemented most of this functionality, but didn't support those captions. You can see an example of these in Figure 12-2.

Figure 12-2. *Buttons without a label caption*

When I added support for the captions, I found I needed a top margin to prevent the captions from running into the content above. That broke the spacing for the buttons with no captions. I decided that maybe I could introduce a class that added some top margin if any of the buttons contained a caption.

The Case for ngOnChanges

At first, I simply dropped the code I needed into a fresh ngOnChanges function, using this code to recalculate the value whenever the input changed.

```
// When the selectableTimes input changes, check for captions
and set a local variable if any are found.
ngOnChanges(changes: SimpleChanges) {
  if (changes.selectableTimes) {
    this.hasCaptions = this.selectableTimes.some(
      (selectableTime) => selectableTime.caption
    );
  }

}
```

It worked, but then it occurred to me that a setter might make more sense. I immediately sent the preceding tweet to get others' opinions.

One commenter suggested that we should use ngOnChanges because "business logic in setters are strange."

Igor made a strong case for ngOnChanges, going so far as posting another twitter thread with sample code. His warning about not using setters if they have to read any other input properties was something I hadn't considered. My use case did not, but it was something to keep in mind.

The opinions kept coming.

Josh said:

> *anything that updates a computed value or needs to react based on multiple inputs, I will use ngOnChanges. For instance, building a slider with min/max inputs...convert min/max to numbers, validate range in ngOnChanges.*

Ryan lent his support for ngOnChanges for my use case, saying that I should use "OnChange for inputs as it feels more visible and correct. I only really used setters for simple things like aliasing form controls etc." The implication is that because I was computing other values from the change, it makes more sense to do as part of a "change" event.

Another response from Rob was to use ngOnChanges to update internal observables that are then bound to the template with async pipes. He didn't provide sample code, but I imagine the change would trigger a new value on an internal RxJS Subject.

Best Practices for Handling Changes to Input Properties in Angular

The Case for Setters

Despite the earlier opinions, I decided to try a setter to see if it looked or felt any better. Using a property setter gave me the direct option to run additional logic whenever the input value changed. Quite frankly, there is little difference between this and the ngOnChanges code, except I don't need a conditional to see what had changed.

```
@Input()
set selectableTimes(value: SelectableTime[]) {
  this._selectableTimes = value;
  this.hasCaptions = value.some(
    (selectableTime) => selectableTime.caption
  );
}
```

What Did Others Think?

Many people simply replied "setters" without explanation. This is fine, as it's what I asked for. Some added that setters look cleaner, citing the fact that with ngOnChanges, you have to have some sort of conditional to determine exactly what changed.

Ashish prefers setters for this case, particularly because it "takes away the extra check to identify what changed... Also code readability and clear intent."

Aissaoui pointed out that setters trigger on your Input changes, but ngOnchange will trigger on all of inputs [changed].

This pattern was pretty consistent across those favoring setters.

How Many Inputs?

Ben pointed out that the decision may depend on the number of inputs your component has.

He went on to add that "setters may fire in an unpredictable order...if you need to control the order across multiple inputs, or you need the value of multiple inputs, then use ngOnChanges."

This warning was repeated by others.

Use a Component Store

Jason suggested not using Inputs at all but use some sort of component store. In fact, the number of suggestions to use a component store may have outnumbered the rest entirely. For my simple use case, I felt this would be overkill.

Property Change Notification?

This appears to be a missing feature in Angular, as pointed out by Rob. Jay pointed out an npm package he built (`www.npmjs.com/package/@trellisorg/update`) to fill this functional gap. As he describes it, it "Provides a decorator (@Update) that allows you to hook into the assignment of a property in a class and then call some function on an injectable to update it."

This appears to be an elegant solution. If I find myself needing this type of functionality more broadly, I may try it.

Observable Inputs

A few people made the comment that we could use Observables with our inputs, which could then be directly piped within the component for additional processing. The resulting Observables would then be available for consumption anywhere in the template with little additional effort.

I would consider this approach for a component that has application context logic, but in this case, I'm building something little more than a reusable widget, so I didn't want to build those kinds of smarts into it.

My Solution

What did I ultimately decide to do? If you look back at my use case, it was simple enough that I could have gone with any of these approaches. In the end, I decided to go with none of them.

I realized that the hosting component has all the knowledge it needs *at compile* time, so it would be the best authority of when to set this extra CSS class.

```
@Input() showCaptions: boolean;
```

My final code simply adds a new @Input to the component that is set by the user of the component. I was able to remove all the additional logic and ship a simpler component.

Summary

It's important to carefully consider the best approach for handling changes to input properties in your Angular components. While both property setters and the ngOnChanges lifecycle hook have their advantages and disadvantages, it's possible to overthink the problem and end up complicating your solution unnecessarily.

If you find yourself struggling to decide which approach is best for your use case, it can be helpful to step back and consider whether a simpler solution might be sufficient. Remember, the key is to choose an approach that is effective, maintainable, and easy to understand for yourself and your team.

PART II

Testing and Debugging

CHAPTER 13

Test-Driven Development with Angular

I tried something "new" recently. I built an Angular service in a true TDD fashion. I wrote the tests first, discovering the service interface along the way. This is how it went. I invite you to follow along.

Background

I admit that I am often not a fan of writing unit tests for Angular apps. The tooling I am using (Jasmine and Karma) feel like afterthoughts. They work and they have gotten much better over the past few years, but they still seem like they were written to bolt onto Angular, rather than being built as part of the ecosystem.

Then I started thinking that maybe the problem is with me. Maybe I despise writing tests because I have not truly adopted test-driven-development in my Angular apps. I used to use TDD all the time with .NET and C#.

So, I decided to go back to that philosophy and build a modest service using strict TDD principles. This is how it went.

© Michael D. Callaghan 2024
M. D. Callaghan, *Angular for Business*, https://doi.org/10.1007/978-1-4842-9609-7_13

The Service

The service itself is simple enough. I want to build a means of setting and retrieving two different unique IDs my app can use when making service calls. The first is a "conversation ID" that will be set as an HTTP header for all network calls for a specific user for a given session. It will not change until the application user manually refreshes the screen, closes the browser, or logs out and back in.

The second is the "correlation ID." This will also get sent with each HTTP call, but it changes with every request.

Not only will these IDs be set as custom HTTP headers on all web requests, they will be logged with all such requests and responses. They can then be used to correlate several layers of service requests and responses back to the user and high-level function that initiated them.

The name of my service is simply correlation. I created it with this Angular CLI command:

```
npx ng g service services/correlation/Correlation
CREATE src/app/services/correlation/correlation.service.spec.ts
(382 bytes)
CREATE src/app/services/correlation/correlation.service.ts
(140 bytes)
```

This creates two files in their own folder at `./src/app/services/correlation`. I got a nearly empty service file and a test (spec) file with one test.

As I usually do, pre-pending npx causes the system to use the locally installed Angular CLI.

The Generated Test

I want to start by reviewing the test code that was generated by the Angular CLI. I do not mean for this to be a comprehensive introduction to testing, but I will explain the basics. It should be enough for you to follow along and also modify your own tests.

```
import { TestBed } from "@angular/core/testing";
import { CorrelationService } from "./correlation.service";

describe("CorrelationService", () => {
  let service: CorrelationService;

  beforeEach(() => {
    TestBed.configureTestingModule({});
    service = TestBed.inject(CorrelationService);
  });
  it("should be created", () => {
    expect(service).toBeTruthy();
  });
});
```

The first import line brings in the Angular testing class called TestBed. This class contains most of the basic testing framework.

The second pulls in the service to be tested, also known as the "System Under Test," or SUT.

Understanding describe

With most JavaScript testing frameworks, tests are organized into one or more describe functions. These can be nested, as you will see shortly.

The describe function is called with at least two parameters:

- The test label. In this case, the name of the service to be tested.

- The function that contains the tests themselves. Here it is an arrow function.

This function contains a single variable representing the service, but nothing is assigned to it yet.

Grasping beforeEach

Directly inside this function is another function call, beforeEach, which itself contains another arrow function. This function is called by the testing framework before every unit test.

This one calls the TestBed.configureTestingModule({}), and you can see that it is being passed an empty object as its only argument. This is the option, and can accept just about everything a normal Angular module can. Most tests use this to configure Angular's dependency injection system to inject test doubles required by the SUT. My service has no dependencies, so there is nothing to configure.

Other Important Functions

Not shown are some other functions that can contain setup/tear-down instructions:

- beforeAll: called once before any tests are run.

- afterAll: called once after all tests have been run.

- afterEach: called after each unit test function.

Understanding `it`

This function defines a single unit test. You can create as many `it` functions as you want inside your `describe`. The generated test comes with a single `it` function. Its signature matches that of `describe`, in that it takes a label and a function defining the test.

When combined with its enclosing `describe`, the `it` functions should read like this:

```
[describe Label] [it Label]: Pass/Fail
```

Thus, when you read the one generated test, it should look like this:

```
CorrelationService should be created: Pass
```

Consider this phrasing when you create your own tests.

There is a lot more to Angular testing than this, but I wanted to make sure I explained what you would be seeing in the following before I began.

Understanding the Service

There are three primary things I need the service to do for me:

- Give me the same conversation ID whenever I ask, unless one does not exist. In that case, it needs to give me a new one and return it.

- Give me a fresh correlation ID every time I request one. I should never get the same ID twice.

- Provide a way for me to force a fresh conversation ID.

These rules allowed me to come up with the following tests. I'm using Jasmine as my testing framework. I know a lot of people these days are using Jest, but the concepts should be the same regardless of what you use.

```typescript
import { TestBed } from "@angular/core/testing";
import { CorrelationService } from "./correlation.service";

describe("CorrelationService", () => {
  let service: CorrelationService;

  beforeEach(() => {
    TestBed.configureTestingModule({});
    service = TestBed.inject(CorrelationService);
  });

  it("should be created", () => {
    expect(service).toBeTruthy();
  });

  describe("resetConversationId", () => {
    it("should return different values on subsequent
    calls", () => {
      const firstId = service.resetConversationId();
      const secondId = service.resetConversationId();
      expect(firstId).not.toEqual(secondId);
    });
  });

  describe("getConversationId", () => {
    it("should return identical values on subsequent
    calls", () => {
      service.resetConversationId();
      const firstId = service.getConversationId();
      const secondId = service.getConversationId();
      expect(firstId).toEqual(secondId);
    });
  });
```

```
describe("getCorrelationId", () => {
  it("should return different values on subsequent
  calls", () => {
    const firstId = service.getCorrelationId();
    const secondId = service.getCorrelationId();
    expect(firstId).not.toEqual(secondId);
  });
});
});
```

Even if you are not intimately familiar with Angular testing in Jasmine, I think these tests are easily understood.

However, these tests won't run and they won't even compile because the functions on the service don't exist yet.

Implementing Auto-Generated Service Code

Fortunately, VS Code will do the heavy lifting for me. All I have to do is put my edit cursor on one of the function names, click the yellow light-bulb (for Auto Fix), and choose "Add all missing members," as show n in Figure 13-1.

```
describe('resetConversationId', () => {
  it('should return different values on subsequent calls', () => {
    const firstId = service.resetConversationId();
    const secondId = service.resetConversationId();
```

| Declare method 'resetConversationId' |
| Declare property 'resetConversationId' |
| **Add all missing members** |
| Add index signature for property 'resetConversationId' |
| Learn more about JS/TS refactorings |

```
describe('getConversationId', () => {
  it('should return identical values on subsequent calls', () => {
    service.resetConversationId();
    const firstId = service.getConversationId();
    const secondId = service.getConversationId();
    expect(firstId).not.toEqual(secondId);
  });
});
```

Figure 13-1. *Auto import in VS Code*

The code it builds is not ideal and will still require some editing, but at this point, the tests will compile.

```
import { Injectable } from "@angular/core";
@Injectable({
  providedIn: "root",
})
export class CorrelationService {
  resetConversationId() {
    throw new Error("Method not implemented.");
  }

  getConversationId() {
    throw new Error("Method not implemented.");
  }

  getCorrelationId() {
    throw new Error("Method not implemented.");
  }

  constructor() {}
}
```

Make Them Run (and Fail)

Now I have code that compiles, implemented in such a way that all three tests will fail with an expected exception. The first thing I need to do is remove the exceptions. My class now looks like this:

```
export class CorrelationService {
  resetConversationId() {}

  getConversationId() {}

  getCorrelationId() {}

  constructor() {}
}
```

I am afraid one of those tests will now pass, but should not. Each function call in the test code evaluates to undefined. This causes the test should return identical values on subsequent calls to pass, because undefined equals undefined.

I will have to edit the tests. I have two choices. I can add three more tests to ensure that no function returns undefined or I can add a check for undefined in the test that is checking for equality.

Some purists believe that every test should have a single assertion/expectation. I tend to be more of a pragmatist. If you are testing one high level "thing," then it is fine to have multiple expectations in a single test.

The new test now looks like this, and fails as expected.

```
describe("getConversationId", () => {
  it("should return identical values on subsequent calls", () => {

    service.resetConversationId();
    const firstId = service.getConversationId();
    const secondId = service.getConversationId();
```

```
    expect(firstId).toBeDefined(); // New code
    expect(firstId).toEqual(secondId);
  });

});
```

Note I am only checking on the first result to be defined. If the first call is defined and the second is not, the second expectation will then fail. I will let you decide which approach makes sense for your project.

Make Them Pass

According to TDD principles, the next step is to write the least amount of code that will cause the tests to pass. In theory, I should not have to touch the tests again. In practice, I probably will. This is a path of discovery, which I am writing as I go. Thus, you are learning right along with me.

```
resetConversationId() {
  return 'mike';
}
getConversationId() {
  return 'mike';
}
getCorrelationId() {
  return 'mike';
}
```

Technically, this will make the middle test pass, but not the others. It is time to think about how the service is supposed to work.

UUID

The business rules call for some sort of semi-unique identifier string. I plan to use a GUID or some variant thereof.

After a few seconds (OK, a minute or so) of research, I found the UUID npm package (raw URL: www.npmjs.com/package/uuid). I will use it to generate both my conversation and correlation IDs.

Once the package is installed in my project, the CorrelationService now looks like this:

```
import { Injectable } from "@angular/core";
import { v4 as uuidv4 } from "uuid";

@Injectable({
  providedIn: "root",
})
export class CorrelationService {
  resetConversationId() {
    return uuidv4();
  }
  getConversationId() {
    return uuidv4();
  }
  getCorrelationId() {
    return uuidv4();
  }
  constructor() {}
}
```

Now the tests pass or fail as expected.

Make It Right

This code looks pretty good, almost complete. There are two things I think are missing.

The first is obvious: Subsequent calls to getConversationId need to return the same value. This means I need a place to store the value. There is also the scenario of the ID's initial value. How do we handle that?

I will tackle the second scenario first by modifying getConversationId to return the stored value, and also by modifying resetConversationId to set the stored value. This will cause the tests to fail, but that is why we write them in the first place. Right?

My modified service looks like this:

```
export class CorrelationService {
  conversationId: string;

  resetConversationId() {
    this.conversationId = uuidv4();
    return this.conversationId;
  }
  getConversationId() {
    return this.conversationId;
  }
  getCorrelationId() {
    return uuidv4();
  }
  constructor() {}
}
```

All the tests pass because I had the foresight to call resetConversationId in the test expecting equality. In reality, this was not a good idea. My motive was good, but I do not believe a user should be forced to call resetConversationId before calling getConversationId. That should be up to the code.

So, now I want to remove the call to `resetConversationId` from the test, which will cause that test to fail.

To enable that code to pass again, I need to modify the service to ensure there is a value before returning it.

```
getConversationId() {
  return this.conversationId || this.resetConversationId();
}
```

Now all my tests pass, the service does the modest job it is meant to do, and my test coverage looks good.

The Final Test

Here is the final set of tests.

```
import { TestBed } from "@angular/core/testing";
import { CorrelationService } from "./correlation.service";
fdescribe("CorrelationService", () => {
  let service: CorrelationService;

  beforeEach(() => {
    TestBed.configureTestingModule({});
    service = TestBed.inject(CorrelationService);
  });

  it("should be created", () => {
    expect(service).toBeTruthy();
  });

  describe("resetConversationId", () => {
    it("should return different values on subsequent
    calls", () => {
      const firstId = service.resetConversationId();
      const secondId = service.resetConversationId();
```

```
      expect(firstId).not.toEqual(secondId);
    });
  });
  describe("getConversationId", () => {
    it("should return identical values on subsequent
    calls", () => {
      const firstId = service.getConversationId();
      const secondId = service.getConversationId();
      expect(firstId).toBeDefined();
      expect(firstId).toEqual(secondId);
    });
  });
  describe("getCorrelationId", () => {
    it("should return different values on subsequent
    calls", () => {
      const firstId = service.getCorrelationId();
      const secondId = service.getCorrelationId();
      expect(firstId).not.toEqual(secondId);
    });
  });
});
```

The Final Service

Here is the entire service.

```
import { Injectable } from "@angular/core";
import { v4 as uuidv4 } from "uuid";

@Injectable({
  providedIn: "root",
})
```

```
export class CorrelationService {
  conversationId: string;
  resetConversationId() {
    this.conversationId = uuidv4();
    return this.conversationId;
  }
  getConversationId() {
    return this.conversationId || this.resetConversationId();
  }
  getCorrelationId() {
    return uuidv4();
  }
  constructor() {}
}
```

I probably could also dispense with the empty constructor, but something in the back of my mind is preventing me from deleting it.

Refactoring the Service

After I finished writing this, it occurred to me that there is a better way to initialize the service than with the || in getConversationId. Why not use the constructor to do its job and construct the object and initialize its internal state?

Before

As you may recall, the getConversationId function looks like this:

```
getConversationId() {
  return this.conversationId || this.resetConversationId();
}
```

If the value of this.conversationId is not defined, the conditional "or" will cause the function on the right side to be executed. That function's side-effect is to initialize the value. TypeScript's conditional "short-circuiting" prevents it from being called if this.conversationId already contains a value.

In this case, it is simple enough to follow, but you may be able to imagine that in more complex classes, it may not be.

After

Instead, I will move the call to resetConversationId into the constructor, guaranteeing that this.conversationId will always have a value. Then, I can delete the conditional check from the latter function.

```
constructor() {
  this.resetConversationId();
}
getConversationId() {
  return this.conversationId;

}
```

To me, this is much simpler code and captures the meaning more clearly than before. Anyone looking at this code will understand that the service pre-initializes its state immediately.

The tests still pass, as they should. This is why we write unit tests in the first place, to ensure that changes to the implementation do not break functionality.

Summary

From start to finish, this experiment took me just over two hours to complete (2:30–4:45 PM). I spent another 15 minutes or so doing the preceding refactoring and writing about it.

The tests were easy to write because the service itself did not exist when I began. By describing the tests as I expected them to work, the service API practically wrote itself.

I am not convinced that a more complicated service or a UI component will be as easy to write in this manner, but overall I am pleased with the result.

I will probably continue to develop the project this way and can honestly recommend that everyone should give it a try some time. You may end being pleasantly surprised.

CHAPTER 14

Unit Testing Strategies

Everyone agrees that Test Driven Development (TDD) is a good thing, right? Right? If you agree that tests are important, you probably write a lot of tests. You might even have a code coverage tool that helps you know how much of your code is tested. Great so far. But here is my question. Are you testing the right code? Are you testing your code, or mine?

Test Your Own Code

I have been doing a lot of code reviews lately, and there is one overwhelming pattern I see repeated. There is a lot of testing being done of code that is not part of the system under test (SUT). In other words, the unit test writers are spending too much time writing tests for code that is outside of their control.

Consider the following scenario. Your app makes calls to a back-end web service to retrieve customer data. You need to log each request and response, but you also need to ensure that any private information is stripped from the log. For your first pass, you decide to create a function that looks something like this:

```
function getCustomer(customerId) {
```

```
  return httpService.get("/customers/" + customerId).
  then(function (response) {
    if (response.statusCode === 200) {
      var scrubbed = scrub(response);
      logger.log(scrubbed);
      return response;
    } else {
      logger.error(response);
    }
  });
}
```

How Do You Test That Function?

There are a number of problems with that function, which make it very difficult to test. As I am fond of telling anyone who will listen: if your code is hard to test, it is probably an indication of a design problem. Let us take a look at why this function is hard to test.

- It relies on an HTTP Service (httpService).

- It relies on a logger.

- It makes an assumption that the response object contains a status code.

- It passes the raw HTTP response to the scrub function.

- It returns a promise.

- It simply does too much.

It Relies on an HTTP Service and Logger

To test this function as written, you would at least need to mock the httpService and logger. There are plenty of ways to do that, but I argue that it is unnecessary at best, and counter-productive at worst.

It Passes the Raw HTTP Response to the Scrub Function

This is related to the prior one. It is also pretty easy to fix. Why does the scrub function need to know anything about HTTP responses? Consider insulating all of your HTTP responses from the functions that use the data. Instead of passing the raw response, extract the pertinent data from the response, and pass that to the scrub function.

It Makes an Assumption That the Response Object Contains a Status Code

Do not make your functions any smarter than they have to be. This tiny function is already much larger than it should be, and testing it appropriately requires more effort than is warranted. If we break the function into its constituent parts, testing the application logic will become much simpler.

It Returns a Promise

This one really isn't too bad. Modern JavaScript testing frameworks make it far simpler to test promises than it used to be. However, it is far simpler to test the asynchronous and synchronous functions in isolation.

It Does Too Much

The getCustomer function does not adhere to the Single Responsibility Principle. Yes, it gets the customer from a back-end service. Then it scrubs the private data from the service's response, which is obviously a good thing in today's privacy-minded society. Scrubbing the data is a synchronous call, and by itself should be easily testable. Then it returns the original unscrubbed response to the caller, whom we can assume needs this data.

Refactor Time

Let us rewrite the function into its constituent parts and see how we might create more testable code.

```
function getCustomer(customerId) {
  return httpService.get('/customers/' + customerId)
    .then(processResponse);
}
function processResponse(response) {
  if (response.statusCode === 200) {
    return handleSuccess(response.data)
  } else {
    return handleError(response.err)
  }
}
function handleSuccess(data) {
  logger.log(scrub(data));
  return data;
}
```

```
function handleError(error) {
  logger.error(error);
  return {};
}
function scrub(data) {
  // Remove Private Information (PII) from data
  ...
  return newData;
}
```

What Have We Done?

First, getCustomer is still the entry point into this particular piece of functionality. Any calling client need not be concerned with these changes, as the public interface hasn't changed.

You might be thinking that this is still hard to test, and you will still end up mocking the httpService and logger to get to 100% coverage. However, 100% Test coverage should not be your goal. Instead, your goal should be to test *your* code. Testing someone else's code is counterproductive. Don't do it.

What Tests Do We Need?

I submit that there is no need to write a test for getCustomer. All it does is make an HTTP call and delegate the result to processResponse. Do you need to test that the HTTP service works? I do not see why. Save that for testing the error conditions you are likely to receive, to ensure they are handled appropriately.

The `processResponse` Function

So, let us start with `processResponse`.

`processResponse` still assumes four things:

1. The response object being passed to it has a `.statusCode` property.

2. That a value of 200 means success and anything else is an error.

3. A valid response object has a `.data` property.

4. An invalid response object has a `.error` property.

If you are just testing this function, in isolation, there are a few strategies I recommend employing.

Ideally, I would write two tests (after all, there are two code paths). The first would pass a request object with a status code of 200. The other would pass it without that status code.

Next, I would replace at test time the `handleError` and `handleSuccess` functions with a shim that I can spy on from the test. That way, I am truly only testing the error checking logic. I do not care what those two functions do: I only care that the right one is called.

`handleError` and `handleSuccess` Functions

These are also easily testable in isolation. `handleSuccess` scrubs and logs the data. Those two functions again would be shimmed from the unit test itself, and my test would simply verify that they were indeed called. Then the function returns the unmodified data object. So, my test would pass in a dummy object I could inspect afterwards to ensure that it was returned unaltered.

Likewise, testing `handleError` just needs to ensure that the logger's error function is called.

In both of these functions' tests, if `logger` is an external service that gets injected, it would be an ideal candidate to create a mock logger at test time. It is also fairly easy to mock something with a small API footprint (in this case, `logger` only has `log` and `error` functions exposed). We can mock the service, replacing those two functions with a spy, and ensure they are called at the appropriate time.

The `scrub` Function

Ultimately, the piece of business we really care about in this block of code is the `scrub` function. Writing a test for this one has become almost trivial. It is a side-effect-free function that takes a single object as input, and returns a new object as output.

Summary

Unit testing code does not need to be hard. If you spend some time thinking about what your tests need to accomplish, you can often find ways to refactor the code to make it more testable, and provide tests that are more meaningful.

The ability to mock existing services is a tool that is worth having. And as you can see, I found a place where mocking made testing easier rather than harder.

Before you start mocking everything, consider what it is you are trying to test. Spend some time separating your code from existing code written by others. Then test just your code and call it a day. Your family and coworkers will thank you, because you may end up being a more pleasant person to have around.

By the way, did you notice I don't have to test the promise anymore? That was intentional and it makes testing much simpler.

Diagnosing Random Angular Test Failures

Have you ever had an intermittent or random failure in your unit tests? I did, and I was pulling my hair out trying to discover the problem. In this chapter, I will describe how I finally managed to find the offending tests and solve the problem.

TLDR

Here are the things I discovered during this process:

- Understand that tests run in no particular order, and that is ideally what you want.

- Turn off random execution to help find the culprit.

- If sequential execution does not help, try various random "seed" values until the tests are failing consistently.

- Isolate the failing test or test suite by using fdescribe, fit, xdescribe, and xit to turn tests on or off selectively.

- Pay close attention to asynchronous code and test doubles.

- Ensure your test doubles are typed correctly, especially your mock services.

Longer Explanation

I am using Angular 10 in this specific project, writing unit tests with Jasmine, and running them with Karma.

My Karma-Jasmine configuration when I began was completely empty, meaning I was using the defaults. Not understanding those defaults caused much of my problem. Out of the box, your unit tests are run in a random order. I was vaguely aware of this, but it had completely slipped my mind at the time. If you take nothing else away from my story, remember this: Whenever you experience intermittent or random test failures, you can almost be sure that one test is causing another to break. The trouble is figuring out which combination.

After the First Failure

As soon as I saw my first failure, I naively assumed it was the most recent test I added. Naturally, I removed it. At that point, the failure went away. I spent the next half hour trying to rewrite the "offending" test to figure out how it caused a failure in an unrelated test. The fact that the new test and the failing test were unrelated should have been my first clue that something else was at work here.

Start Disabling Tests

As I write this, my project has 153 unit tests. The failure was occurring in an afterAll function, which I did not even have. The error referred to a specific component, but not a specific test. I could not even determine which test to skip. Instead, I decided to start running a subset of tests by selectively disabling some of the other tests and test suites.

Disable Random Test Ordering

By this point, I was reasonably sure the problem was one test causing a failure in another one. The trick now was to figure out which one. On a whim, I decided to turn off random ordering in the Jasmine configuration. As I said, I am running my tests with the Karma test runner. So, inside the karma.conf.js file, I simply needed to add some Jasmine-specific configuration to the client section.

Before, that section looked like this:

```
client: {
  clearContext: false; // leave Jasmine Spec Runner output
                       visible in browser
}
```

To disable random test order, I added this:

```
client: {
  clearContext: false, // leave Jasmine Spec Runner output
                       visible in browser
  jasmine: {
    random: false
  }
}
```

This would guarantee that my tests would run "in order," starting with the first spec.ts file it finds and then running the tests from top to bottom in each file. It occurred to me that this probably would not reveal any new insights. I was right. All tests passed. The good news is that the test run was now repeatable. Every test run passed now.

Did it solve my problem? Nope, but at least I felt I was making progress.

You Can Specify the Random Seed!

The next thing I did was to turn random ordering back on, but this time provide my own random seed. If you are not familiar with a seed, it is a number used to initialize the random number generator. The benefit of this approach is that using the same value to seed the random number generator will provide the identical sequence of random values on subsequent runs. Thus, once I found a seed that caused my test failure to show itself, I could continue using that seed during my investigation.

I started with the seed 1234. Because I had no idea what value might cause the problem, it really did not matter. On the first run with that value, all the tests passed, so that was no help. I continued changing the seed value until my test failed. Fortunately, it only took me a couple of attempts. I ended up with a configuration like this:

```
client: {
  clearContext: false, // leave Jasmine Spec Runner output
                          visible in browser
  jasmine: {
    random: true,
    seed: '12345'
  }
}
```

Start Isolating Tests

Now that I could reliably reproduce the problem, it was time to start isolating the failed test from the working ones.

On my first attempt, I simply ran only the failing test in that test suite, by changing describe to fdescribe. This block had only one it block, so I was only running a single test from this suite.

As I expected would happen, the test passed. When run in isolation from the other tests in the test suite, it worked just fine.

As a sanity check, I disabled every other test in the project, and as expected, the remaining test passed.

Next, I began turning on one test at a time. I considered turning on half, and then the other half. However, this particular suite only had ten tests in it, so I simply started at the top and turned them on one by one. As luck would have it, the very first test I enabled caused the problematic test to fail.

Now the real investigation began. What code did the first test run that caused the second test to fail?

Give Asynchronous Code a Closer Look

As I looked closer at the failing test, I noticed that it was testing a failure scenario. A passing test actually meant that an error occurred inside my component. This test used the `async/await` pattern to wait on the asynchronous service call it had to make.

I had seen this problem before, and almost certainly knew what had caused it. The function in many of my components that made asynchronous service calls were not returning the promise to the caller. Consider this block of code (not my actual code):

```
// Component function
getSomeData() {
    // Service function
    return this.service.getData()
        .then( data => { ... })
        .catch( error => { ... })
}
```

In this code, the promise returned by `service.getData()` is being returned by the component's `getSomeData()` function to its caller. If you forget to do that, the testing code will have nothing to `await`. My component had many such functions, and I had been meticulously going through them all to make sure they returned the service call's promise. I immediately checked the particular function being exercised by the failing test. To my surprise, it was fine.

That, however, led me to another realization. The test itself was bad. It looked like this:

```
it("should set an error if it throws", async () => {
  // service here is a test double, a mock of the real service
  service.getData.rejects({ message: "test-error" });
  fixture.detectChanges();
  await component.getSomeData();
  expect(component.error).toBeTruthy();

});
```

The testing code was using `async/await`, but had no `try/catch`! I decided that I would rewrite the test without `async/await`, instead using catch. The modified test looked something like this:

```
it("should set an error if it throws", () => {
  // service here is a test double, a mock of the real service
  service.getData.rejects({ message: "test-error" });
  fixture.detectChanges();
  component.getSomeData().catch((err) => {
    expect(component.error).toBeTruthy();
  });

});
```

At last, I was pretty sure I had found the problem. I eagerly enabled all units tests and reran the tests with the same seed I had been using. The problematic test failed again, with the exact same error!

New Test Suite

At this point, I decided to start with a clean slate. I disabled all tests in that component's test suite. Then I used the Angular CLI to create a brand new component, complete with its unit test boilerplate.

Once that was done, I painstakingly began copying tests one at a time from the old test suite into the new one. I started simply, copying just enough code to initialize the component. That test failed due to missing service doubles. Next, I copied those test doubles (mostly service mocks) into the new suite.

With the test doubles in place, my component creation test passed. One down, nine to go.

The next test up was the failing one. It did something only one other test in the suite did. It changed the behavior of one of my mock services. Could that be the piece I had been missing?

Suspect Your Test Doubles

I deleted my test doubles and reentered them individually. While doing this, I noticed that two of my mock services were created as object literals directly in the test suite. This was odd, as I also had a mock service defined as a class in another file. I decided I should try to use that instead.

The code used to look something like this:

```
const service = {
  getData: () => Promise.resolve({data});
}
```

```
providers: [
  { provide: DataService, useValue: service }
]
```

I moved the getData call into my Mock Service and changed the provider to look like this:

```
let service: DataService; // Notice this is strongly-typed now
providers: [{ provide: DataService, useClass: DataService }];
```

I had left in the variable declaration so that I could redefine its behavior in the error path. But now I had a compiler error. This line in my failing test was no longer valid.

```
service.getData.rejects({ message: "test-error" });
```

That is because service was now strongly typed to be a DataService, and getData returned a promise. It had no function named rejects. The solution was to replace the getData function completely, but just for this test.

Recall that I said this test was inside its own describe block, so I added a beforeEach to it, where I could replace the behavior of the getData function to reject instead of resolve the promise. Now my test looked something like this:

```
describe("getSomeData (error path)", () => {
  // Redefine service.getData here, outside the test itself.
  beforeEach(() => {
    service.getData = sinon.stub().rejects({ message: "test-
    error" });
  });
  it("should set an error if it throws", () => {
    // service here is a test double, a mock of the
    real service
```

```
    fixture.detectChanges();
    component.getSomeData().catch((err) => {
      expect(component.error).toBeTruthy();
    });
  });
});
```

Here I am using sinon to create the stub, but you can use a similar strategy with Jasmine's own functions.

The beforeEach on the overall test suite itself creates a brand new instance of the mock service before each test. Then, in this test, its getData function is replaced with a new function that returns a rejected promise instead.

I was feeling pretty good about where this was heading. I enabled all the tests and reran them. All passed. Finally, I removed the seed value from the Jasmine configuration and let the tests run in a random order. The test has been passing ever since.

Summary

I have been careful not to show any of the actual test code that caused my problem, but instead just enough code to get my point across. My goal was to discuss how to isolate the problems in your tests, rather than discuss testing strategy. To that end, I hope I have succeeded.

PART III

The Command Line

CHAPTER 16

Command Line: What Do All Those Symbols Mean?

Do you know about all those weird symbols you can use on the command line?

Even though you might spend most of your time in an interactive development environment (IDE), it's important to understand how to use the command line.

Recently, I saw a tweet suggesting that if you place a single ampersand between two shell commands, they run in parallel. While partially true, the tweet didn't fully explain the whole scenario. So, I thought of revisiting the basics and explaining just what these and other symbols do in a Linux, MacOS, or even Windows (Bash) terminal.

This is the tweet I referred to:

Did you know that a double ampersand && will run multiple scripts sequentially while a single & will run them in parallel?

—Dan Vega (@therealdanvega), April 11, 2019

Note   The examples contained in the following were all tested and work on a macOS terminal running the bash shell. They should work on any other common shell in Linux, and should even work in GitBash for Windows. As always, your mileage may vary.

And &&

Most developers are familiar with this example, especially when dealing with build scripts. For example:

```
npm test && npm run build
```

The common understanding is that this command runs npm test and then npm run build. But that's not quite right. It's more accurate to say that it runs npm test, and only if npm test succeeds (exit code is 0), will it run npm run build. If the first command fails (exit code != 0), then the second command won't run at all. This is typically the behavior you'd want. For instance, in this example, if the tests fail, there is no reason to run the build.

To validate this, try the following in your terminal:

```
ls this-folder-does-not-exist-anywhere && echo "I will not execute"
```

You should see an error message, and the echoed string will not appear. You can chain as many commands as you like using &&, just remember that the first command that fails will interrupt the rest.

Or ||

What if you want the sequence of commands to continue regardless? You might try using the Or (||) operator, but that probably won't work the way you think. While the && operator terminates after the first failure, || terminates after the first success. So, the second command will only run if the first command fails!

Here's a demonstration:

```
echo "I worked" || echo "Which means I will not execute"
```

This construct is often used as a simple test mechanism before creating a file or folder. Consider this example:

```
[ -d ~/i-do-not-exist ] || mkdir ~/i-do-not-exist
```

The first command tests whether a directory exists. Thus, the entire command says, "make this directory, but only if it does not already exist." This method avoids writing an error to the terminal, unlike using ls ~/i-do-not-exist.

My Home Folder ~

If you're unfamiliar with the tilde ~ symbol from the previous example, it's a handy shortcut representing your home directory. Here's how to expand it using the echo command:

```
echo ~
```

Output:

```
/Users/michael
```

Background &

Let's return to the tweet suggesting that a single & allows the commands to run in parallel. While true, it doesn't tell the whole story. Generally, you'd use the & operator when you want a long-running shell script to execute in the background. Sure, you could open another terminal session, but that would use more resources.

Here's an example of a long-running command that searches for all PDF files in my home directory, writing each file's path into a text file named my-pdf-files.txt.

```
find ~ -name *.pdf > ~/my-pdf-files.txt
```

On my i7 MacBook Pro, this command takes over 2.5 minutes to execute. Adding the & operator to the end of that command causes it to run as a background job, allowing you to continue with other tasks.

```
find ~ -name *.pdf > ~/my-pdf-files.txt &
```

On execution, you get an immediate response like this:

```
[1] 35715
```

This output indicates that my background job is Job #1, and its process ID is 35715. You can check its status with the jobs command.

```
jobs
```

Output:

```
[1]+ Running find ~ -name *.pdf > ~/my-pdf-files.txt &
```

You can bring it to the foreground with the fg 1 command, which blocks your terminal. Once in the foreground, you can suspend the job by typing Ctrl+Z, and then typing bg to send it back to the background.

To terminate the process, use the kill 35715 command (the process ID from initial command's output).

How does this work with two commands? If the two commands are related to each other, it probably won't work well. But, if I want to run two similar `find` commands, one looking for PDFs and another for MP3 files, they can run in parallel as it doesn't matter which one completes first.

```
find ~ -name *.pdf > ~/my-pdf-files.txt & find ~ -name *.mp3 >
~/my-mp3-files.txt &
```

Output:

```
[1] 36782
[2] 36783
```

This command creates two background jobs, indicated by the two job numbers and process IDs provided. When they complete, your terminal will display something like this:

```
[1]- Exit 1 find ~ -name *.pdf > ~/my-pdf-files.txt

[2]+ Exit 1 find ~ -name *.mp3 > ~/my-mp3-files.txt
```

Redirect Output >

If you have been following along with these examples, you may have seen a few error messages. Even though the commands are running in the background, the output of both is being displayed at the terminal. That is easy enough to fix, by redirecting its output, using the "greater than" or "right angle bracket" symbol (>). In fact, I used that in the previous two examples.

Using a single > symbol tells the shell to redirect the standard console output (stdout) to the file specified. So the prior `find` command sends its standard output to the file. If the file does not exist, it will be created. If it does exist, it will be replaced.

If you want the command to append to the file instead of creating it from scratch, you can use two >> symbols.

None of that prevents errors from being displayed on the console, because that is a different output stream (known as stderr). You have a couple of alternatives here. You can send the errors into a different file, by specifying another redirect, like this.

```
find ~ -name *.pdf > ~/my-pdf-files.txt 2>~/errors.txt
```

The 2> specifically indicates that you are redirecting stderr. As you might guess, 1> indicates stdout, but the default redirect is stdout, so the 1 can be omitted.

Further complicating things, you can redirect stderr to the same target as stdout, by using &1 as its target, like this:

```
find ~ -name *.pdf > ~/my-pdf-files.txt 2>&1
```

&1, another example of & that means something else entirely, is shortcut for "where stdout is being sent."

I do not often have occasion for stdout and stderr to end up in the same file, particularly in the previous examples, where I am collecting files of a certain type into a file of those files. In those scenarios, I would prefer simply to throw those errors away.

In MacOS or Linux shells, I can choose to redirect stderr to /dev/null, a special file that simply ignores everything. On Windows, I understand there is a special file called nul that accomplishes the same thing.

So my complete command will look like this:

```
find ~ -name *.pdf > ~/my-pdf-files.txt 2>/dev/null
```

Redirect Input <

I see this used less often, as most commands accept the name of an input file as an argument. Back in the day™, many (if not most) commands operated on standard input (stdin), by default, the keyboard, and sent its output to stdout.

Imagine I want to know how many of those PDF files from before were found. I could open the file in my favorite text editor and check, but there is an easier way. I can type this command in the terminal.

```
wc -l < ~/my-pdf-files.txt
```

Result:

```
3308
```

Yeah, I had no idea I have that many. wc is the "word count" command, and the -l switch tells it I only care about the number of lines. By default, wc takes its input from stdin, which you can see by typing the command by itself, entering any text you want, ending your input by typing Ctrl+D.

```
wc -l
```

Input:

```
Mike
was
here
Ctrl+D
```

Result:

```
3
```

Notice that the Ctrl+D isn't counted as a line. It also needs to be specified on a line by itself. If you type it at the end of a line, it will be part of that line.

This strategy works with any command that accepts input from stdin, which is most commands available in the terminal.

One command I see most often is more, which is used to page the output of a file.

```
more < ~/my-pdf-files.txt
```

Again, I do not see this used much anymore; most of these commands accept the file to be operated on as an argument. This version of the command is far more common.

```
more ~/my-pdf-files.txt
```

I/O Pipe |

What about the single | operator? This is an I/O Pipe. It uses the output of the first command as input to the second command. Think of this as a combination of both > and <.

What if I wanted a sorted list of those PDF files? I could use the sort command after the fact. However, I could also use the | pipe as part of the find command, ignoring errors, sorting the output, finally depositing the information in a new file, executing the entire thing as a background job.

```
find ~ -name *.pdf 2>/dev/null | sort > ~/my-pdf-files.txt &
```

Expand $

Every system has environment variables. These are settings specific to the running system. On my Mac, I have more than 100 of them. If you need to use them inside of a shell script or another command, they can be convenient to know about, even when they have a command equivalent.

For example, I mentioned ~ previously. You can also reference that with the $HOME environment variable. On my system, I also have things like $HOSTNAME, $USER.

The outputs of these commands are often used inside of other commands.

```
echo My home directory is \~
echo My home directory is \$HOME
```

A very common use of this is to see what folders on your system are searched for executable files. This is allows you to type java-version instead of its absolute path, which would be much longer and more inconvenient to type.

```
echo \$PATH
```

Expansion Within " "

The preceding echo command is special. It can handle multiple parameters. Most commands prefer you to surround a string like that in quotes, to be considered a single parameter. In that case, it is important to know the difference between single quotes (') and double quotes (").

When you use double quotes, your environment variables will be expanded.

```
echo \"Hi, \$USER! Have you cleaned up your \$HOME folder
today?\"
```

Output:

```
Hi, michael! Have you cleaned up your /Users/michael folder today?
```

In this command, the $USER and $HOME variables are both expanded. The entire string is passed as a single parameter to the echo command.

No Expansion Within ' '

If you do not want the environment variables to be expanded, you can use single quotes instead (').

```
echo \'Hi, \$USER! Have you cleaned up your \$HOME folder
today?\'
```

Output:

```
Hi, \$USER! Have you cleaned up your \$HOME folder today?
```

Use Command Output ''

What if you want to execute a command and include its output as part of another command? For that, you can surround the command with back-ticks (`). This is different from output piping, as it is not necessarily redirecting the output of one command as the input to another command. Consider this overly simplistic example.

```
echo \"You have \`wc -l \< \~/my-pdf-files.txt\` PDF files.\"
```

Output:

```
You have 3308 PDF files.
```

The wc command is executed, its output is placed into the string at that point, and then the entire string is passed to the echo command.

Another place I use this pattern often is trying to find the actual location of an executable. On my Mac, most executables are symbolically linked into the /usr/bin folder. So this command does not provide the information I need.

```
which java
```

Output:

```
java is /usr/bin/java
```

To know where it really is, I will use the ls -l command on the output of the which java command, like so.

```
ls -l \`which -p java\`
```

The -p switch shortens the output to just the path, without the message "java is". On my system, this expands to the command I really want to run.

```
ls -l /usr/bin/java
```

Output:

```
lrwxr-xr-x 1 root wheel 74B Sep 11 2018 /usr/bin/java -\> /System/
Library/Frameworks/JavaVM.framework/Versions/Current/Commands/java
```

History!

The last symbol I want to mention is the exclamation mark, or bang (!). This symbol allows you to execute any command in your command history. To see a list of these commands, enter the following command.

```
history
```

Output:

```
657 which -p java
658 ls -l \`which -p java\`
659 history
```

You will be presented with a possibly lengthy list of commands, with the most recent at the end of the list. To execute any of them, simply type the bang followed by the command number shown next to the command.

```
!657
```

Output:

```
which -p java
/usr/bin/java
```

You can use the grep utility to search your history. For example, here are all the find commands I ran while writing this chapter, piped through the uniq utility to get only unique commands.

```
history \| grep find \| uniq
```

Output:

```
585 find \~ -name \*.pdf \> \~/my-pdf-files.txt
586 find \~ -name \*.pdf \> \~/my-pdf-files.txt &
589 find \~ -name \*.pdf \> \~/my-pdf-files.txt & find \~ -name
\*.mp3 \> \~/my-mp3-files.txt &
605 find \~ -name \*.pdf 2\>/dev/null \| sort \> \~/my-pdf-
files.txt
606 find \~/Downloads/ -name \*.pdf 2\>/dev/null \| sort \> \~/
my-pdf-files.txt
608 find \~/Downloads/ -name \*.pdf 2\>/dev/null \| sort \> \~/
my-pdf-files.txt &
663 history \| grep find \| uniq
```

Ctrl+R Search History

As a bonus, in some shells, you can also use the keyboard shortcut Ctrl+R to search your history interactively. To see this in action, type Ctrl+R followed by the text of a command, for example, find. The most recent match will appear. Continue typing Ctrl+R to step backwards through the history. At any point, you can stop by pressing Space, or the right or left arrow keys. You are then free to edit the command, pressing Enter to execute it. Press Ctrl+C to get out of the history without doing anything.

Summary

Even though they are specifically targeted to *nix-based OSes, many of these work in GitBash or similar on Windows.

I have only scratched the surface of the special symbols available in many terminal shells.

PART IV

Source Control

CHAPTER 17

Source Control: In Search of a Better Code Review

How to Set Up GitHub to Smooth Your Team's Development Process

Source control is of vital importance in modern software development. As a developer, you need to be confident that you can recover from mistakenly deleting your code. It should be easy to create "what if" experiments that are trivial to undo if necessary. Also, developers rarely work alone. A good source control system makes it convenient to work with others and incorporate their changes into your code, and vice versa.

There are plenty of opinions about the best way to handle code reviews and pull requests on a software project. Some teams and companies are very strict, requiring multiple levels of reviewers and only a few people authorized to perform merges. Other teams are at the opposite extreme, allowing anyone to merge their branches at any time with no oversight whatsoever. In this chapter, I will propose something in the middle.

© Michael D. Callaghan 2024
M. D. Callaghan, *Angular for Business*, https://doi.org/10.1007/978-1-4842-9609-7_17

The Problem

In one of my projects, there were few developers and only a single authorized code reviewer (ACR). The ACR was the only person with write permissions to the protected branch, develop in our case. Thus, he was the only person who could approve and merge feature branches into develop. Interestingly, though the ACR was a member of the team, he was not assigned any development responsibilities on the project. He had responsibilities to other projects, so his time was understandably dedicated to those projects primarily. The feature development process had feature branches created and pushed to origin, with pull requests following. At that point, the pull requests would back up, waiting for days or sometimes even weeks to be reviewed.

There were not enough developers on this particular project to enlist others to help with development or code reviews, and it got frustrating quickly.

I decided to research a more efficient and effective process.

Goals and Constraints

My goals are to reduce the time it takes for a pull request to be opened, reviewed, and merged with our main development branch.

Some of my constraints are that code is hosted on an internal GitHub instance in private repositories. This limits the pool of potential reviewers.

Recommendation

If you simply want to see my recommendation, you can read this section and stop. The remainder of the chapter will be my supporting arguments and reasoning, which led me to this recommendation.

Development Work Flow

This is a sample code flow I envision for any given feature:

- A developer (Pat) is assigned a new feature.

- Pat creates a new branch (FB) from the HEAD of the "main" branch (or whatever it is called in your repository). Note: Pat does not fork the repository, but has write access to it.

- Pat implements the feature into FB, using as many commits as necessary.

- When complete, Pat pushes FB to origin and opens a pull request.

- Pushing FB automatically starts a build of FB, and the build status is reported back to the repository.

- If the build fails, the system will not permit FB to be merged.

- The repo contains a PULL_REQUEST_TEMPLATE.md file, which encourages consistency in pull request descriptions.

- Pat requests that two or more peers review the pull request.

- The "Code Owner" for the repository is automatically assigned to review the pull request.

- If any reviewer requests changes with the code review, Pat cannot continue with the pull request until those changes are addressed.

- Once the changes are addressed, Pat pushes new commits to FB, at which time all existing reviews are dismissed, and the process begins again.

- If the main branch is updated while the pull request is open, Pat must merge those changes into FB before it can be merged.

- This cycle is repeated until all reviewers have approved, FB is consistent with the main branch, and all builds of FB pass.

- At this point, Pat is free to merge the pull request and delete FB.

GitHub Protected-Branch Settings

Here is a description of my recommended settings for protecting the base branch. Figure 17-1 shows them all together, after which I will describe them in more detail.

Protect matching branches

☑ **Require pull request reviews before merging**
When enabled, all commits must be made to a non-protected branch and submitted via a pull request with the required number of approving reviews and no changes requested before it can be merged into a branch that matches this rule.

> Required approving reviews: 2 ▾

☑ **Dismiss stale pull request approvals when new commits are pushed**
New reviewable commits pushed to a matching branch will dismiss pull request review approvals.

☑ **Require review from Code Owners**
Require an approved review in pull requests including files with a designated code owner.

☐ **Restrict who can dismiss pull request reviews**
Specify people or teams allowed to dismiss pull request reviews.

☑ **Require status checks to pass before merging**
Choose which status checks must pass before branches can be merged into a branch that matches this rule. When enabled, commits must first be pushed to another branch, then merged or pushed directly to a branch that matches this rule after status checks have passed.

☑ **Require branches to be up to date before merging**
This ensures pull requests targeting a matching branch have been tested with the latest code. This setting will not take effect unless at least one status check is enabled (see below).

> Status checks found in the last week for this repository
>
> ☑ continuous-integration/jenkins   `Required`

☐ **Require signed commits**
Commits pushed to matching branches must have verified signatures.

☑ **Require linear history**
Prevent merge commits from being pushed to matching branches.

Figure 17-1. *My recommended GitHub protected-branch settings*

The Rationale

This section contains a more detailed explanation of the preceding workflow.

A Single Protected Branch

I propose protecting a single branch, in our case the develop branch, which is where all our feature branches get merged into. This can be known as the "main" branch, the "base" branch, etc. I use all three terms interchangeably.

Write Access for the Entire Team

In order for this recommendation to work effectively, each member of the team must have write access to the repository. This enables a feature branch to be created directly in the repository, rather than forcing developers to fork the repository. The benefit is that code reviewers can easily pull the feature branch onto their own machine for testing (if necessary), instead of having to clone the forked repository. Using forked repositories was common in the past, before the introduction of protected branches. It still is common practice in open source projects, where features can be contributed by virtually anyone. In a corporate setting, the latter use case is unlikely.

Pull Request with Template

Each repository should include a pull request template file (named PULL_ REQUEST_TEMPLATE.md) to help keep pull request descriptions consistent between features and developers. At a minimum, the template should prompt the developer for the following information:

- A link to the "user story" or issue that the pull request addresses.
- A high level summary of the changes.

- A quick start on how to build and test the branch. Remember, some reviewers may be from another team and may not be intimately familiar with the project.

- What to look for in the application.

Optional

The pull request template may also contain prompts for these items:

- Test and Linting results (though this can be managed by the status checks).

- Screenshots of the current implementation UI, if relevant.

- Any additional context to help review and test the pull request.

Authorized Reviewers

This is where things get interesting. I propose following the model of an external company, pullrequest.com. They use code reviewers who are completely removed from the project, and even the company requesting the reviews. These reviewers provide a fresh perspective unavailable from those doing active development on the project. Such individuals need only read access to the repository.

The primary benefit to this is numbers. More potential reviewers implies a faster time to first comment, which results in quicker pull request turnaround.

In addition, every developer on the project should be an authorized reviewer.

Given that all our reviewers have access to the corporate network, we can take an additional step. We should allow and encourage our reviewers to clone the repo, and then build and run the application from the feature branch.

A useful side-effect of including reviewers from outside the immediate team is that it helps to avoid siloed knowledge. At any time in the future, reviewers could potentially be tapped to join the project, either temporarily or permanently, and not come into the project blind.

Strict Status Checks

In our case, we are integrated with a Jenkins build pipeline. All branches pushed to `origin` are built, code analysis is performed, and all unit tests are run. The status of this build and test phase are reported back to GitHub and the pull request containing that branch. Before collaborators can merge changes into the protected branch, this build must completely succeed.

Require FB to Be Up-to-Date with the Main Branch

The feature branch in a pull request will need to be up to date after other collaborators merge pull requests to the protected base branch. This puts the burden of merge conflicts onto the feature developer, the person closest to the code and most likely to resolve them quickly.

Required Code Owner Review

Each project should have one or more "code owners" who are not part of the development team. They could be technical managers, development leads from another project, or senior architects. The code owners are specified by providing a CODEOWNERS file in the root folder of the base branch. The interesting thing about this approach is that different code owners can be assigned for different file types, branches, etc. The details of whom to be assigned as code owner can be determined by the project team.

The code owners' responsibilities will not be to review the code in detail, but simply to review the other reviews to ensure that they have been completed satisfactorily. Once the appropriate code owners have reviewed and approved the pull request, no additional reviews are required.

Require Linear History (Use Squash Merges from Feature Branches to Main Branch)

This recommendation is all about reverting features in case problems are discovered later. If a protected branch requires a linear history, then only squash or rebase merges are permitted. I recommend the former. When a squash merge is performed as part of a pull request, the entire feature branch is merged into the base branch with a single commit. While it is a "best practice" to make multiple commits during development, this can lead to more difficult merge conflicts for developers on other branches. Using a squash merge from a feature branch to the base branch will reduce the feature to a single commit, making it easier for other developers to pull those changes into their own feature branches. It also helps in the event that the feature branch needs to be reverted. Providing a single reverse commit can undo the entire pull request, if it becomes necessary to remove a feature from an upcoming release.

Merge Completed by Code Author

When all reviews and status checks are complete, it is up to the original feature branch author to perform the merge and delete the feature branch if desired. Whether or not you delete feature branches is a decision best left to the development team. I like deleting them and keeping the origin clean, but some teams prefer to keep them around.

What About Automatic Merge?

GitHub has an option to merge automatically once all other gates are passed. I am tempted to recommend that, but I would only push for it if it turns out the build/test/deploy cycle is too lengthy.

Summary

I hope this has been helpful. You may or may not agree with some of my suggestions, which is fine. What I hope to have impressed upon you is that code review and pull request policies are flexible in GitHub. Your team should discuss what will work best for your project based on your developers' experience and needs.

If nothing else, I hope you will have enough information to have the conversation.

CHAPTER 18

Fix Mistaken Git Commits

Recently one of my development teams had a merge problem. For version control, they use a modified form of GitFlow (`https://nvie.com/posts/a-successful-git-branching-model/`), and it was time to merge from the develop branch to the release branch. If things are done correctly, this should always be a clean, simple merge. It is especially true in this case because it was their first release for a new project. The team opened a pull request from develop to release and then reported to me that GitHub was reporting merge conflicts. Huh? How is that possible? The release branch should be empty. Except that it wasn't.

As it turned out, a well-meaning developer on the team knew that the code eventually needed to go into release, so that's he committed all his changes. Locking down branches is a topic for another day, I suppose. I had to deal with the problem in front of me first.

I ran the following command on the release branch.

```
git log --oneline
```

Its output showed something like this:

```
1 852291a blah blah blah
2 f575c87 blah blah
3 83d855d blah blah
```

© Michael D. Callaghan 2024
M. D. Callaghan, *Angular for Business*, https://doi.org/10.1007/978-1-4842-9609-7_18

```
4  9fa11df blah blah blah blah
5  111b003 blah blah
6  2b3a530 blah blah blah
7  a4c5f54 blah blah blah blah blah blah
8  b2a62fa blah blah blah blah blah blah blah blah blah
9  5fb67b9 blah blah blah
10 4d1a5fc blah blah blah
11 ed40aec Initial commit
```

No, we really don't use "blah blah" as commit messages. As I said, these commits were made directly to the release branch, and not through a merge or pull request from develop, which is the prescribed method. I don't hold any grudges against the well-intended developer. Both Git and this workflow are new to that team, and I mostly blame myself for not at least setting up a 30-minute discussion ahead of time. They weren't new to source control, just this particular process.

Regardless of my feelings or the good intentions of the team, I was faced with a problem I had to solve. A new pull request from develop to release was waiting. The test team was waiting for a release build, and that wasn't happening. I decided that the best and safest thing to do was to undo each of those commits.

So after a bit of Google- and Bing-foo, I landed on some questions and answers at StackOverflow (about:blank) that enabled me to find just the right sequence of Git commands to fix the release branch. I include the experience here in the hopes it may help you someday.

The first thing I had to do was figure out how to revert a series of commits. There were only 11, so I could have done them one at a time, but what if there had been 111 instead? I wanted to understand the process regardless of the number of commits. After reviewing the various commands that are available, I settled on the following syntax:

```
git revert --no-edit <oldest-commit-hash>..<newest-commit-hash>
```

This actually took a few tries, because most of the documentation said things like "first bad commit" and "last bad commit." Is "first" the oldest, or is it #1 in the log? Turns out, it's the oldest, which is the highest number in the commit log.

So, to undo all of those commits in the aforementioned list, I used the following command:

```
git revert --no-edit ed40aec..852291a
```

The –no-edit flag kept Git from prompting me to edit the commit message for each of the 11 reverse commits it made. Instead, it used the original commit message, preceded by the word "Revert." Fine by me. After that command completed, each of my commits had a mirrored revert, in reverse order. Checking the directory showed that the only thing present was the initial README.md file. Perfect! So the only thing left to do was push the branch back up to the server:

```
git push origin release
```

Back on the server, I checked the open pull request from develop to release, and there were no merge conflicts. I completed the pull request, and the build was able to continue.

Now the testers can get on with their work, and we can all live happily ever after – until the next problem, of course.

Summary

Hopefully, reverting a huge series of commits isn't something you need to do often. However, if you do find yourself in a similar situation, remember that it's entirely possible to regain control and restore order. We faced an unexpected situation where a release branch contained numerous direct commits instead of simply being updated through a pull request from the develop branch. Using the git revert command, we successfully undid these problematic commits and achieved a smooth pull request and build.

CHAPTER 19

Archive Your Git Repository

Did you know there is a very simple and straightforward command to archive a complete Git repository, while including no historical information? Here I will explain both how and why I do it.

Why Archive Your Git Repo?

Every few weeks or so, I find myself needing to archive my Git repo. Often I do this to send code to someone who has no reason to access the repo directly. They just need a snapshot of the code, with no history information, because they won't be contributing to it.

I also provide a snapshot of my code for every module in my Pluralsight courses (`https://bit.ly/ps-mike`). Being able to archive my Git repo into a zip file is very handy.

For some reason, I can never remember how to do this, and find myself looking it up repeatedly.

© Michael D. Callaghan 2024
M. D. Callaghan, *Angular for Business*, https://doi.org/10.1007/978-1-4842-9609-7_19

How to Do It

If you want to back up a Git repo, completely detaching it from Git, use one of the following variations of the git archive command:

Zip File

```
git archive --format zip --output /full/path/to/zipfile.
zip master
```

Tar File

```
git archive master > /some/other/path/my-repo.tar
```

Tar/Bzip

```
git archive master | bzip2 > my-repo.tar.bz2
```

In each of these cases, the word master is the branch I am archiving. You can archive any branch you want, simply by replacing master with the name of your desired branch.

Though not strictly necessary, I like to create my archive from the root of my repo, and have my archive created outside of it.

Note   The archive will not contain the .git directory, but will contain other hidden git-specific files like .gitignore, .gitattributes, etc.

Summary

In this chapter, I talk about the how and why of archiving a Git repository without its history. I often need to send code snapshots to people who don't need access to the full repo, or for my Pluralsight courses. I share three variations of the `git archive` command to create zip, tar, or tar/bzip archives. Despite its simplicity, I find myself frequently forgetting these commands, so I've documented them here. The archive won't include the .git directory but will have other Git-specific hidden files. I also provide a Stack Overflow link for additional info.

Reference

- `https://stackoverflow.com/questions/160608/do-a-git-export-like-svn-export`

CHAPTER 20

Use "git-bisect" to Find Problems Fast

Recently I noticed that one of the styles on a custom component got messed up. The component consists of a piece of text between two icons. There used to be some generous space between the icons and the text, but now there isn't, as you can see in Figure 20-1.

Figure 20-1. *Stepper buttons with no spacing*

I first suspected that a class had been changed. Maybe it had some padding and now it doesn't, but a quick check in the Chrome Developer Tools showed no such padding in the production version (which still looks right).

It became apparent that I broke it somewhere over the past week or so. I commit often, so looking through each commit would be laborious and time-consuming. If only there were a way to narrow down the commits and go through them logically and methodically.

Well, with git-bisect, there is!

© Michael D. Callaghan 2024
M. D. Callaghan, *Angular for Business*, https://doi.org/10.1007/978-1-4842-9609-7_20

git-bisect to the Rescue

What is git-bisect? It's a clever and little-used utility that will let you blast through a series of commits by cutting the commits in half, testing the app, and then repeating the process.

Here's how it works, and how I used it.

First, find a commit somewhere in the past where you know for a fact that code worked. Copy this commit's hash. It will be your starting point. The other end of the bisect is your HEAD commit, the one you know is broken.

I had to look through my git log to find the commit that originally included my code. I ran `git log --- oneline | head -25` to see my last 25 commits. I found the one where I first implemented the code that is now broken, remembering it was working at the time. I made note of its commit hash, 2d8cf845.

Armed with this information, I entered the following commands:

```
git bisect start
git bisect good 2d8cf845
git bisect bad HEAD
```

The first command initializes git-bisect, but otherwise doesn't do anything. The second command tells git that I know that commit was good. My final command indicates a commit that I know doesn't work: my bad commit. Instead of providing a commit hash, I simply used HEAD, which is my most recent commit.

The output from git-bisect tells me there are six revisions or commits between those two, and that it should take me three steps to find the culprit.

Run the App

Now it's time to run the app and see if the problem exists. My issue is visual, so I'll have to build and run the app and inspect the output.

It looks perfect. You can see the spacing between the number 1 and the icons in Figure 20-2.

Figure 20-2. *Stepper buttons with desired spacing*

So, now I tell git that this is a good commit.

```
git bisect good
```

Notice that I only needed to tell git-bisect that this commit is good. It then automatically selected a commit between that one and my bad one and checked it out for me.

I rebuilt and refreshed the app, and that one was also good.

This one was also good, so I repeated the aforementioned command.

The command output tells me that there are zero revisions and zero steps left, so this had better be the bad one, which it turned out to be.

With git-bisect's help, I only had to try three commits to find the culprit.

Had it not been my final commit, I would have marked it with `git bisect bad`, and then git would have continued narrowing down the changes until we finally found the offender.

Find the Bug

Now that I have the commit, I can look at the diff and find out what I might have done to break it.

I loaded the project in GitHub and navigated to that commit. Fortunately, my commits aren't very big and I quickly spotted the problem. The custom component uses a third party flex layout library, which is required for the components to render correctly. For some reason I cannot recall, I had removed the inclusion of that library from my main set of scripts.

Replacing that single deleted line solved my problem. Being the good team player that I am, I created a new fix branch and opened a pull request with that single-line change.

Summary

Finding an unexpected bug is never a good feeling. It's even worse when you can't remember touching the code that broke. In my case, I had made the change haphazardly, thinking I was deleting an unused import. I was wrong.

Fortunately, I was able to use git-bisect to find the problem commit, identify the change that caused the break, and issue a correction. This entire experience, start-to-finish, took me about half an hour, including the time I spent keeping notes and writing up this explanation.

There is a lot more to git-bisect that what I've shown you here. If you have unit tests, and you're trying to find the commit that broke one or more of them, it's even possible to have git-bisect do most of the work for you. It can run your tests and decide for itself whether the commit was good or bad. That's an advanced topic for another day.

Hopefully, the next time you find yourself in a similar predicament, you'll remember this chapter and try git-bisect yourself.

PART V

Communication and Training

CHAPTER 21

How We Learn

Have you ever stopped to think about how we learn things? I was recently reflecting on this topic when my 15-year-old was learning to drive. I had the unenviable job of teaching him. At the time, it struck me that he had to think about every little detail of what he was doing. He needed to be reminded to check his mirrors, signal his lane changes, look behind him when backing up, etc. Learning to drive requires absolute and complete attention. He didn't even have the spare mental capacity to listen to music.

Watching him struggle reminded me of something I learned many years ago about how we learn new things. Regardless of what we are learning – whether it's driving, putting up drywall, or learning a new programming language – we all go through four stages of learning. You could think of them as the four steps of mastery. They are

- Unconscious incompetence: You don't know what you don't know.

- Conscious incompetence: You understand what you don't know and want to learn.

- Conscious competence: You start to understand, with effort.

- Unconscious competence: You internalize your understanding and no longer have to think about it. You just "get it."

© Michael D. Callaghan 2024
M. D. Callaghan, *Angular for Business*, https://doi.org/10.1007/978-1-4842-9609-7_21

Learning to Drive

In my son's case, Step 1 occurred when he realized he wanted to drive, but had no idea what that entails. This is the stage where every little detail needs to be explained. Progress is slow, but as long as he has enthusiasm for the subject, we move forward.

Learning Mobile App Development

Likewise, you may decide that you want to learn mobile app development, but don't know where to begin. This is Step 1, unconscious incompetence. You may not even know what technologies are available to help you. But you're excited about a new idea you had that will change the world.

So you do some research, read some online blogs, talk to friends and colleagues, and perhaps pick a place to start. You understand pretty well that there is much you still have to learn. You at least know what you don't know, and have now reached Step 2, or conscious incompetence. This is the prime learning stage. You read more specific articles, maybe take some classes, or watch training videos.

Applying Knowledge to Practice

If you're like most people, this isn't quite enough. You have begun to understand the material on an intellectual level. Now you need to practice, apply what you've learned. After doing this awhile, you finally reach Step 3, or conscious competence. Your skills are improving, but you aren't completely comfortable yet. This is the time when you slowly become accustomed to the new skill, but still occasionally need to appeal to your local experts, refer to reference material, or post to Stack Overflow.

Mastery

As you continue to practice and apply your knowledge, eventually you'll discover that you no longer need to look up the syntax of an obscure feature or the parameters of troublesome functions. You may also realize that you are answering more questions than you're asking. Congratulations. You've reached Step 4, unconscious competence, the ultimate pinnacle of mastery.

Depending on the subject, you may be satisfied to stop at Step 3. It may not be possible to go further. That's OK. It isn't necessary or even desirable to master every subject or every skill.

Time and Learning

You may have noticed that I haven't said anything about the time this takes. That depends on many factors: your personal or professional interest in the subject, the time you have to spend on this compared to other demands, or how well you have learned to learn. That's right, you go through these same steps even when learning to learn.

Summary

What should you take away from this? Keep these steps in mind the next time you start to learn a new skill. And in the meantime, practice your learning. Pick a topic. Study it. Pay attention to the steps you go through.

In the next chapter, I discuss how these same steps can apply from a different perspective: that of a teacher. I will show how the teacher's approach has to change, according to which step the student is on.

CHAPTER 22

How We Teach

Knowing the basics of how to teach is critical on the path to becoming an effective Angular Advocate.

In the previous chapter, I specifically discussed the four steps that everyone goes through when learning something new. In this chapter, I am going to discuss how to teach students at each step of the process. The techniques used vary, depending on where a given student is. Please note, you don't have to be a professional teacher to understand and use these techniques. Whether you are a teacher, a parent, a manager, a mentor, or even a student yourself, understanding these techniques can make you better at what you do.

To recap the four stages learning, they are

- Unconscious incompetence: You don't know what you don't know.

- Conscious incompetence: You understand what you don't know and want to learn.

- Conscious competence: You start to understand, with effort.

- Unconscious competence: You internalize your understanding and no longer have to think about it. You just "get it."

© Michael D. Callaghan 2024
M. D. Callaghan, *Angular for Business*, https://doi.org/10.1007/978-1-4842-9609-7_22

Teaching EDGE

The Boy Scouts of America is widely recognized as an organization that is expert at teaching practical skills to millions of boys (and now, girls), using mostly volunteers with very little training. They do that by using the teaching methods I am going to describe here. Those methods are wrapped in something they call EDGE.

EDGE is an acronym that stands for Explain, Demonstrate, Guide, and Enable. Each of these represents a specific teaching style, applied in order to help anyone learn a new topic or skill. It's not a coincidence that there are four steps, and each one aligns perfectly with the four stages of the learning process.

Explain

When students are on Stage 1, unconscious incompetence, they don't know what they don't know. It's up to you Explain everything to them. If the material is brand new, you cannot assume that they will have even basic knowledge of the subject. Everything needs to be spelled out. You should avoid acronyms and jargon, especially anything that is specific to the subject being taught. Explaining the subject moves the student closer to Stage 2, conscious incompetence.

Demonstrate

Once the subject has been explained, and it appears that the students understand the basics of what's going on, you can move onto Demonstrate.

Here you have the opportunity to offer a practical demonstration of the topic, skill, or task being taught. Depending on the complexity of the topic, more than one demonstration, along with repeating the explanation for reinforcement, may be necessary. This is Stage 2, conscious incompetence. They understand what it is they do not know.

Through demonstration, you provide a visual, sometimes hands-on, illustration of the idea you are trying to convey.

Guide

Now it's time to practice. With your help, the student takes a turn exercising the skill or applying the knowledge provided. During this phase, you will carefully Guide the student every step of the way. This step is cyclical, and repetition will almost certainly be required. Continue to explain as needed, and perhaps go back to demonstrating a particular technique. With practice, the student will gradually move to becoming consciously competent. The skill won't be automatic yet, but understanding is there.

Enable

Once you feel that the student has a solid grasp of the concepts you are teaching, it's time to back off and give them a little space. You gradually remove your immediate supervision, to Enable the student to master the subject. One way to do that is to have the student informally teach someone else the same topic or skill. Teaching others reinforces those concepts and helps move the individual towards unconscious competence.

Example

Let's look at a real-world example of using EDGE in practice. As I mentioned in the last chapter, I had been experiencing the delightful process of teaching my 15-year-old son to drive. EDGE is incredibly valuable here. During one lesson, we practiced panic braking. One Saturday morning, we found an empty parking lot behind an office building, and prepared for the lesson.

The first thing I did was Explain to him what we would be doing. We discussed when panic braking would be necessary, and how to do it safely, with and without anti-lock brakes. (Notice I did not assume he knew the acronym ABS.) We talked about how to steer a car while braking, where the driver's attention should be focused, etc.

Once the Explanation was finished, I proceeded to Demonstrate the techniques we discussed. I showed him panic braking from various speeds from 15 to 35 miles per hour.

Then it was his turn. We switched places, and he practiced what I had just demonstrated. I did not simply hand him the keys, get out of the car, and let him drive off. Instead, I remained with him to Guide him through the process, answering questions, gently correcting him when necessary, and offering helpful reminders when appropriate.

It would be foolish to assume at this point that my son has totally mastered this skill. I will Enable his progress by providing opportunities for him to continue practicing and gaining confidence.

Challenges

There are some tactical challenges to be aware of. EDGE works best when there is something tangible to demonstrate and practice. It would be difficult to teach world history using EDGE. You would be hard pressed to get much past Explain and Demonstrate. I am not sure how you Guide someone through a practical history lesson. What is important is to realize that each step in the process reinforces the previous one. The further you and the student can go, the better.

Another potential challenge is that most people do not learn at identical rates. If you find yourself teaching a group, you will quickly discover that they will not all pick it up at the same time. You need to be patient, often repeating steps based on where the student is. That is why understanding the equivalence between EDGE and the steps of learning is key.

A final challenge is that many students, myself included, have a hard time picking up a new concept that has no immediate application in their lives. In other words, some people have a hard time learning just for the sake of learning. As a case in point, I struggled for years to learn how to tie certain Boy Scout knots. This was particularly embarrassing while I was serving as a scoutmaster. On one campout, however, I was given the task of securing our flagpole to another pole. I knew I had to lash the two poles together. I even knew that I had to use a Round Lashing. I had simply never been able to do it. One of the scouts saved me by teaching me, using the EDGE method, how to use the clove hitch and round lashing to secure the two poles together. Once I had a "why," I was able to master the skill relatively quickly. Round lashings and clove hitches no longer give me any trouble.

Summary

Whenever you find yourself teaching someone a new topic or skill, whether formally or informally, your student will certainly go through the steps of the learning process. Being able to recognize which step they are in, and to respond with the appropriate EDGE technique, will make you a more effective teacher. Your students will learn faster and retain the information better. With practice, you may even be able to have your student teach the next student, which serves to reinforce the knowledge in both the student and the teacher.

CHAPTER 23

Slow Down to Be Noticed

If you want to have a more positive impact on those around you in your daily life, personal or professional, I have two words of advice: slow down. I will explain the details and benefits in this chapter.

Background

I get asked from time to time what kinds of advice I have for people looking to get ahead, be taken seriously, or just be thought of more positively. After an experience I had with some young men at church, one of my favorite suggestions is to recommend they try slowing down their speech.

Though the following events happened in a religious setting, the principles I will describe apply equally in personal, academic, and professional settings. Allow me to set the stage.

I was facilitating a Sunday meeting at church with some of our older teenagers. We were taking turns reading scripture and it seemed that everyone, myself included, was simply going through the motions. We heard the words, but there was little meaning being conveyed.

An Idea Took Shape

I stopped everyone and suggested that we start over, but this time with a twist. I chose one of the young men and asked him to read a somewhat lengthy verse in his normal cadence, while I timed him. I asked the rest of them to close their eyes and just listen. His time, as I recall, was somewhere around 25 seconds.

Then I asked him to read the same verse again, but this time as slowly as he could without feeling uncomfortable. I asked the others to close their eyes and listen once more, and again I timed him. It was less than 35 seconds. Longer, but not dramatically so.

The result, however, was very dramatic. The mood in the room changed. Everyone sat still, absorbing a scripture passage they had now heard three times. It seemed to take on an entirely new meaning.

In fact, it was close to magic.

The boys then took turns with this experiment. Though each read and spoke much more slowly than normal, none sounded unnatural or forced. Their words were clear and distinct, each syllable perfectly enunciated.

By the end of the experiment, each was convinced that there was something to this. I challenged them to try to apply this in their everyday lives. In school, read more slowly and with greater intent. Also try to speak more slowly and clearly. I promised them that if they made a conscious effort, then they would see positive results. They accepted.

Demonstration

Reading about this experience will only provide you with half of the story. I want you to understand what I am telling you at a deeper level.

To demonstrate, I recorded myself reading the Preamble to the US Constitution (see Figure 23-1) three different ways. I assure that throughout the recordings, I have not used any editing to speed up or slow down the content.

Figure 23-1. *US Constitution*

Obviously, you cannot see the videos here. You can view them on YouTube with this link: `https://bit.ly/wr-slow-down`.

Normal

At first, I simply read the words at a comfortable pace, without trying to go slower or faster than I normally would. It took me just about 19 seconds to read at this pace. I believe it is understandable.

Fast

On the next pass I read the passage as fast I could without the words becoming garbled and meaningless. This took about 12 seconds to get through it. Though the words are reasonably clear, it strikes me that the overall message is lost.

Slow

The final reading is my attempt to go as slow as I comfortably could, paying attention to each word, and speaking as clearly as possible. I timed this at 24 seconds. To me, it does not sound forced or intentionally prolonged. It sounded worse in my head while I was reading it than it sounds to me now.

Result

What do you think? Can you hear, and possibly even feel, the difference? I hope you agree that the final reading is the most impactful and imparts the greatest meaning to the listener.

How You Can Apply This

My reason for telling you this story is to convince you to apply it in your own life, both personal and professional.

Most of the people I work with tend to speak too quickly and too loudly, myself included. Whether you are reading or speaking, intentionally slow yourself down. Hear each word as you speak it. Pay particular attention to enunciating the consonants. If you can do so naturally, try to use fewer contractions. Say "cannot" and "will not" instead of "can't" and "won't." And please, try never to use the word "could've." It too often comes out sounding like "could of," which is not even a proper phrase.

Speaking more slowly has the additional effect of causing us to speak more softly. I do not quite understand why this is, but it seems universal.

If you decide to try it yourself, I predict that you will experience some benefits almost immediately.

People Will Listen

When you speak softly, slowly, and clearly, people will pay more attention to what you are saying. Perhaps it is counter-intuitive, but you will be heard more the quieter you are. That does not mean to whisper. If you find that people are asking you to repeat yourself, you are probably speaking a bit too quietly.

People Will Notice

A few weeks after my experiment with our young men, I heard from some other members of our congregation. They reported that their interactions with these young men had improved significantly, but they struggled to tell me exactly why. They knew the boys were doing something differently, but they could not say what.

I concluded from their comments that people will notice something has changed for the better, but they will probably not know exactly what the change was.

Try It Yourself

Choose a similar passage of text that is important to you and conduct your own experiment. Read it three times, as I did previously. Record yourself and play it back. Time it. Find out how it sounds after a brief delay to reset your brain.

Once you have convinced yourself that there is something to this, apply it in your daily life. Maybe start at home, deliberately trying to slow yourself down when you speak and read. Tell no one for at least a week. See whether or not people begin treating you differently, maybe with a little more respect. Report back and let me know how it goes.

Summary

In this chapter, I tried to impress upon you the power of slowing down, particularly in the way we speak and read. To illustrate the point, I recorded myself reading the Preamble to the US Constitution at different speeds. The slowest reading, which was also the most deliberate, had the most impact.

I challenge you to apply this technique in your daily life. Whether you're in a meeting or having a casual conversation, slowing down your speech can make you more understandable and impactful. It also tends to make you speak more softly, which paradoxically makes people pay more attention.

I encourage you to try this experiment with a text that matters to you. Observe the changes in how people respond to you. Hopefully if you do so, you should be convinced of the benefits of slowing down and be equipped to implement this simple yet powerful change in your life.

CHAPTER 24

Watch Your Language

Pay attention to your language, spelling, and grammar in your speech, writing, and emails.

At the risk of offending some of my peers, I wish to make an observation. As a group, we tend to be horrible at written communication. Software developers are some of the worst writers I have ever read. We make sloppy mistakes, both in spelling and in grammar. Whether you write technical articles for a living, blog posts for a hobby, or pull request comments, this chapter is an attempt to provide some simple guidance to improve your language and your writing.

Profanity

Allow me to get this one out of the way early. Though it has become more acceptable in society, profanity has no place in a professional setting or in your professional writing. If you are writing a novel, or perhaps an article for *Rolling Stone*, swear all you like. Please do not swear in your technical tutorials, blog posts, and especially not your business emails. Profanity makes you appear neither smarter nor more mature.

© Michael D. Callaghan 2024
M. D. Callaghan, *Angular for Business*, https://doi.org/10.1007/978-1-4842-9609-7_24

Spelling

First and foremost, use a spell checker. In today's world, there is no excuse for spelling words incorrectly. However, if you are not careful, you can still use a correctly spelled word incorrectly. In the following are some common mistakes I see often.

Alright

There is no such word, even though many spell checkers do not flag it. It is an informal form of all right.

Alot

This word does not appear in the English language. It is an informal way of saying a lot. When in doubt, consider using many.

Do not use

- There were alot of bugs in the last release.

Instead use

- There were a lot of bugs in the last release.
- There were many bugs in the last release.

Cancelled/Canceled

Though technically either form is correct, in most of the English-speaking world, the proper spelling is canceled. Quite frankly, it does not matter which one you use; try to be consistent.

Irregardless

Again, there is no such word. There are two words you may wish to use instead: regardless or irrespective.

October 2020 Update!

It was brought to my attention by Team 33 Productions on Twitter (https://twitter.com/33ProductionsSP) that I am indeed mistaken about this. Evidently irregardless is a word, as reported by NPR in July 2020 (www.npr.org/2020/07/07/887649010/regardless-of-what-you-think-irregardless-is-a-word).

That said, I concur with the following, taken from the article:

"It's not a real word. I don't care what the dictionary says," responds author Michelle Ray, who teaches English in Silver Spring, Md.

I stand by my recommendation that you should not use the word.

It's/Its

This one probably bothers me more than any other. The word it's is a contraction, meaning it is. The correct possessive form is its.

Do not use

- My cat just spent the last five minutes chasing it's tail.

- Its a beautiful day outside.

Instead use

- My cat just spent the last five minutes chasing its tail.

- It's a beautiful day outside.

Let's/Lets

I see this one often. The word let's is a contraction meaning "let us." On the other hand, lets is a verb meaning "allows."

Do not use

- I hope the manager let's us use Ionic.

- Lets try Ionic for this project.

Instead use

- I hope the manager lets us use Ionic.

- Let's try Ionic for this project.

Then/Than

I think this one confuses people because we no longer use then in most programming languages for conditionals. Shell script and BASIC programmers probably do not make this mistake.

Then follows if. Than is used to compare two things.

- If this, then that.

- This is better than that.

There/Their/They're

Their defense is over there working hard to show they're the most talented.

Whose/Who's

Whose is possessive. "Whose pull request is this?" However, who's is a contraction meaning who is. "Who's responsible for this new feature?"

Your/You're

Your is possessive. You're is a contraction meaning you are. Please do not confuse the two. Whenever I see your welcome in a message, I always want to reply, my welcome what???

I imagine that this is almost always a typo, but it is worth mentioning.

Grammar

Even though you may spell words correctly, and use the correct spelling of your words, it is possible to confuse your reader by using inappropriate language, words, and grammar. This section contains the errors I see most often.

Awhile/A While

I admit to being guilty of this one myself. A `while` refers to an indefinite amount of time. `Awhile` is an adverb, and will usually appear next to a verb. Also, though some people do it, do not use `awhile` after a preposition.

Do not use

- The code took awhile to build.

- We should discuss our build process for awhile.

Instead use

- The code took a while to build.

- We should discuss our build process awhile.

Imply/Infer

If you expect your reader to derive some meaning from your statement, you are implying. Your reader is inferring. Try not to reverse them.

Lead/Led

The past-tense of the verb lead is led, often confused with its homonym lead, which is a metal.

Less/Fewer

I see this error often, and the rule is pretty simple. If you can count something, use fewer. If you cannot count it, or you tend to use its singular noun form, use less.

Do not use

- This code release has less bugs than the last one.

Instead use

- This code release has fewer bugs than the last one.

- This code release is less complex than the last one.

Split Infinitives

An infinitive is a verb form that is used as a noun. The word replicate is a verb. To replicate is a noun. In the sentence Docker enables teams to replicate, the verb is enables and the noun is to replicate.

Splitting an infinitive involves adding another word between the two.

Do not use

- Docker enables teams to quickly replicate their development and production environments.

Instead use

- Docker enables teams to replicate their development and production environments quickly.

Also correct, though less common:

- Docker enables teams quickly to replicate their development and production environments.

Though splitting infinitives is becoming more acceptable and widespread, especially in informal writing, the use of split infinitives seems lazy.

Contractions

Some two-word phrases are commonly abbreviated into contractions (can't, shouldn't, we're, they'll, etc.). Most of us who are not Lt. Commander Data use them almost unconsciously. This is not a hard and fast rule, so much as a preference on my part. I was taught many years ago that one should avoid using contractions in professional and technical writing. Their use is considered too informal.

Do not use

- It's come to my attention that you're having questions, and don't understand why we're doing this project.

Instead use

- It has come to my attention that you are having questions, and do not understand why we are doing this project.

Summary

Like it or not, people do judge you based on your words. Sloppy writing is unprofessional. Spend some time making sure that your meaning conveys your intent.

If you made it this far, then you probably experienced at least one of two emotions:

- Slight embarrassment that I exposed some flaw in your own writing style.

- Annoyance at one or more of my opinions.

If you agree with me entirely and make none of these mistakes, congratulations!

If you have some favorites of your own that I have forgotten, or you believe I made any spelling or grammatical errors myself, please let me know.

PART VI

Other Topics

Agile Software Development: A Quick Start Guide

The Basics of Agile Software Development and How It Can Benefit Your Project

A recent tweet of mine seemed to get a lot of traction, so I decided to revisit an article from a few years ago, updated for today's software development needs.

Agile software development is a popular and effective way to build software. It emphasizes collaboration, flexibility, and regular delivery of working software. In this blog post, we'll introduce you to the basics of agile and explain how it can improve your team's software development process.

When starting a new software project, your team has a lot of decisions to make. Not the least of which is how to track the features from initial design through completion. Agile can help make the entire process easy and painless. Let's jump right in.

For the purposes of this chapter, I'm going to use Trello. If you want to follow along, doing so with Trello will be the simplest way, but you should be able to apply the ideas to any similar tracking system.

Task Creation and Tracking

Setup with Trello is fast. Simply go to the Trello website at www.trello.com/, logon (or create an account), create an organization for your team, add members, and set up a new board. By default, your board will include three empty lists, like the one shown in Figure 25-1:

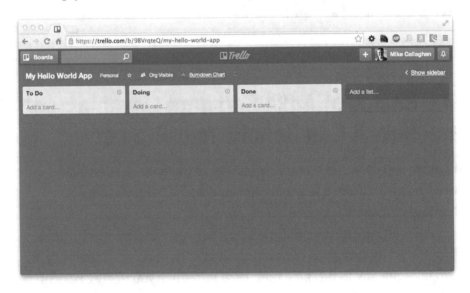

Figure 25-1. *Trello Start Page*

Though your lists can be modified at any time, this is a great place to start, and will allow you to create a backlog of stories and tasks quickly, without regard to importance, how long a task might take to accomplish, or who will end up implementing them.

Every feature and idea that anyone has is fair game at this stage. Create a new card in the "To Do" list for every idea, user story, or task you can think of, as shown in Figure 25-2.

As long as a card is in this list, anyone can make changes to it. Cards can be moved around at will, but should be sorted by importance. The more important cards are near the top. This forces you to make value judgments on the relative importance of your features. Because cards must be in order, no two cards can share the same significance. This eliminates the problem of every feature request being considered "critical." The most critical card is always the one on top.

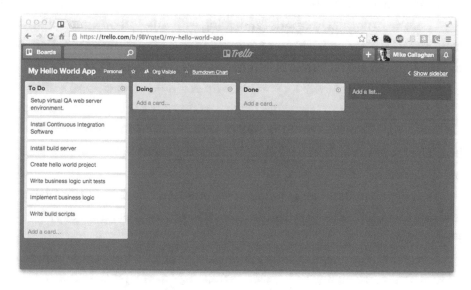

Figure 25-2.   *Trello board with To Do items*

All changes and comments to all cards are logged, so it's easy to look back and see a history of how a feature has evolved over time.

Estimation

Estimates are important for planning and prioritizing work, even though they may not be completely accurate. As a project progresses, teams can use actual data and experience to refine their estimates and make them more accurate. By tracking progress against estimates, teams can identify potential issues and adjust their plans accordingly. Overall, estimates are a valuable tool for managing software development projects.

Most agile tracking tools have estimation capabilities included, but Trello has no built-in mechanism for estimating the time any particular card will take to complete.

There are informal methods for dealing with this, but one particularly clever idea is to use a web browser extension to make it painless for the entire team. Scrum for Trello is a free browser extension for Chrome, Firefox, and Safari that will let you place an estimate on each card's title.

Once the extension is installed, you can simply click on a card's title to set its estimate. A small row of numbers appears just under the title's text box. The numbers are the typical agile planning values from 0 to 21. Click on one to set it.

Your development team should go through each card in the To Do list and assign an estimate. Very simple tasks will probably get a 0.5 or 1. See Figure 25-3.

Extremely complicated tasks might get a 13 or 21. Those cards should be broken down into multiple cards so that every estimate is a single-digit number.

Figure 25-3. *Trello Board with Scrum for Trello Estimates*

By design, the numbers do not contain units. They don't represent any particular measure of time.

Most Agile practitioners call them story points. For now, don't get hung up on what the numbers mean. They won't be accurate at the beginning even if you try. The important thing is that the developers are comfortable that each card has a value that is accurate, relative to the other cards in the list.

You will notice that the Scrum extension adds up the estimates for each card and displays the total at the top of the list, as well as the total of all cards on the board.

Iteration Planning and Scheduling

Now it is time to start planning and scheduling your actual development work. You will want to agree with your team on a set period of time in which your work will be accomplished. Most Agile methodologies refer to this as an "iteration" or "sprint." It doesn't matter what you call it, and I will use the former term here.

The typical length of an iteration is two weeks, though some teams like to use one or three. One week iterations can work well for highly efficient teams doing very small tasks. Three week iterations work well for some teams, though I find it too long between planning and feedback.

This is also where you may want to consider making your first custom list in Trello. I like to create a new list between To Do and Doing. Simply click the "Add a list…" link to the right of your right-most list. Call it "Current Iteration." Create the list and drag it to the space between To Do and Doing. This is where the current work will go.

Your task at this point is to select the most important cards from the To Do list, and move them to the Current Iteration list, as you can see in Figure 25-4.

Remember that cards should already be organized by importance from top to bottom, so you simply need to drag them from one list to the other. As you do so, the Scrum extension will update the list's estimate. Continue dragging cards until the developers feel confident that they can complete the amount of work scheduled.

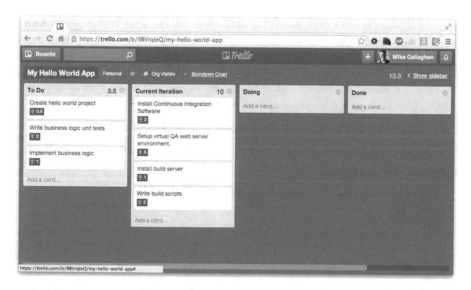

Figure 25-4. *Trello Board showing work scheduled in the current iteration*

Developers should not be pressured to accept more work than they feel they can handle, especially in your first iteration.

Development

Once your iteration is planned and cards are in the Current Iteration list, development work can begin. There are now a few rules that must be strictly enforced during the development phase. One is that no one is allowed to change any card's description or estimate. Another is that no cards be moved between the To Do and Current Iterations lists, with one exception that I will address shortly. These rules and a few more are summarized at the end of this post.

At the beginning of every day, the developers should get together to discuss what cards they intend to work on that day. No two developers can work on the same card simultaneously. Doing so indicates that there is more than one task on that card, and it should be split into multiple cards. You can do that if necessary, but be sure that the total estimate doesn't change.

As developers select a card to work on for the day, they will assign the card to themselves (select the card, click Members, and add themselves). Then the developer will move the card from Current Iteration to Doing, and begin to implement the feature on the card, an example of which can be seen in Figure 25-5.

Throughout development, comments and checklists can be freely added to the card.

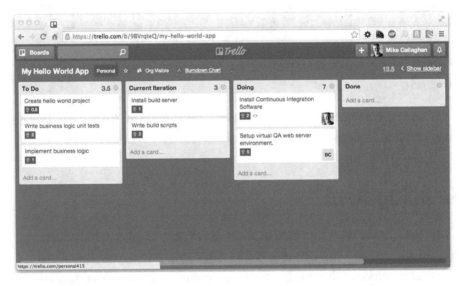

Figure 25-5. *Trello Board showing work in progress*

The powerful thing about this is that everyone on the team can see the current state of development at any time at a glance, simply by loading the project's board. The boards update automatically when anything changes, so that all users see others' changes almost immediately.

If a developer has a question for someone else on the team, he can enter that question as a comment on the card, tagging the individual(s) expected to have the answer. Those tagged in a card will be pro-actively notified by Trello.

When the developer has finished implementing a particular card, drag it from Doing to Done. He can then take another card from Current Iteration, assign himself to it, and drag it to Doing. Developers continue to work in this way until the iteration ends or they run out of cards.

Running out of cards is the exception to the rule of not moving cards between To Do and Current Iteration, as I show in Figure 25-6. This simply indicates that the developers are working faster than initially expected. If this happens, management (in consultation with developers) should move one or more cards from To Do into Current Iteration, again based on importance. The developers can continue working until the iteration ends.

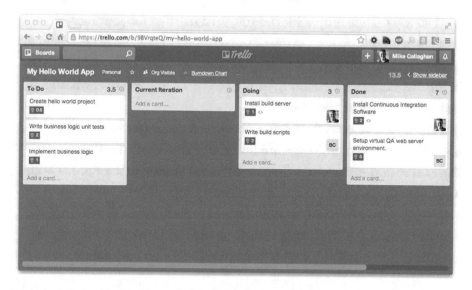

Figure 25-6. *Trello Board showing no work left to do*

If the iteration ends with cards still in the Current Iteration list, don't consider it a failure of your estimation or planning. It just means you put in more cards than the developers were able to finish. This is important information that you can now use to help plan the next iteration.

Calculating Velocity

At the end of your iteration, look at the number at the top of the Done list. This is your "velocity" for this iteration. Whatever that number is, use it as your number to plan the next iteration. For example, if the number at the top of Done is 150, then for your next iteration planning, try to plan cards so that your total estimate does not exceed 150. This is the reason you shouldn't concern yourself with each estimate's units. If you planned for 120 and the actual is 125, then your velocity is 125. Plan for 125 next time.

Likewise, if you only achieved 100, then use that for your next iteration's plan. It doesn't matter if the numbers represent hours, days, or something else entirely. That's why using an arbitrary term such as "story points" works so well. No one gets bogged down arguing over whether a task will take one or two hours.

Track your velocity from iteration to iteration. As each iteration completes, you will probably find that your planning and estimates get better. If your numbers vary drastically from iteration to iteration, it is an indication that something else may be affecting your velocity. A lower velocity may be a hint that something is hampering your developers' effectiveness. A slightly higher velocity could indicate that your team is starting to get comfortable with the process and with each other.

Individual Velocity

Another metric you can track is velocity by developer. To determine each developer's individual velocity, simply add the story points of each card completed by each developer. This can be of tremendous value if your developers don't work the same number of hours each week on your project.

Let's say you are using two-week iterations, you have two full-time developers and one part-time. Plus you have an intern who works whenever he can. After a few iterations, your two full-time developers have average individual velocities of 50 and 55. Your part-time developer is averaging 20. And your intern averages 10. If you also know that your part-time developer is only working three days per week, you can assign him 20/6 or 3 1/3 "points" per day. The intern is working one day per week on your project, so you assign him 5 points per day. The two full-time developers also get roughly 5 points per day.

Once you've calculated individual velocities, it becomes a trivial task to see which of your developers is most effective. In my example, the part-time developer has a lower velocity than the rest. The others are all about the same.

This being a contrived example, I won't go into why some developers will have a higher velocity than others. There are many reasons for this, and only a few of them have anything to do with one developer being "better" than others.

Continuing the example, imagine that one of your developers will be on vacation for half of the next iteration. Knowing his velocity is 5 points per day, you can simply remove 25 points from your next iteration's maximum. If the intern gets an extra day next week, you can schedule another 5 points.

Bugs and Testing

Your iterations should include cards for testing and bug fixes. Bugs should be treated no differently than other cards. If bugs are found during or after an iteration, they need to be added to the To Do list as individual cards, estimated, and scheduled into the next iteration. If the bug is truly exceptional and critical to finish in the current iteration, you may swap the bug fix for an existing card already scheduled, but not currently being worked on.

It is crucial that you do not add bugs to the Current Iteration unless you remove enough cards equal to the estimate of the bugs you are adding.

The overall estimate of the Current Iteration cannot change in the middle of an iteration. Sometimes you may be tempted to force a higher velocity on your team by adding more work hours or asking the developers to work harder, but that tactic will only work in the short-term, and is likely to backfire on you.

Rinse and Repeat

At the end of every iteration, schedule a period of time (an hour or two) to review the work that was completed. This is the iteration's retrospective, where you will calculate and discuss your team's velocity. It is a good time to have a "start, stop, and continue" review to determine what worked and didn't during the iteration, and what things can be improved for the next iteration [raw URL: www.people-results.com/start-stop-continue/].

Figure 25-7 shows a completed iteration, with nothing left to do. This is the ideal scenario. That won't always be the case, though. Any cards remaining in the Current Iteration can be left there for the next iteration, or if management decides, can be put back into the To Do list for reevaluation. The same goes with cards in the Doing list, though because work has already started, it would be a waste to move them back into the To Do list.

All cards in the Done list can be archived. Alternatively, you can rename the Done list with the current iteration number, and then archive the entire list. If you choose this route, simply create a new Done list to be used with the next iteration.

Figure 25-7. *Trello Board showing a completed iteration*

Once you have completed the retrospective, you can roll right into the planning for your next iteration, and repeat the process.

Summary

Once you become accustomed to working in this manner with Trello, you should find that your planning sessions become more productive, management will always know the state of the work being done, and developers will argue less over their estimates and work assigned to them. Eventually you will reach a state of predictable releases, which will make everyone happy.

Rules to Live By

As I mentioned earlier, there are a few rules that everyone needs to agree to if you want to make this work. Many agile tracking systems can help enforce these rules. Other than logging all changes, Trello won't. It's up to the team to be professional and agree to stick to them.

- Anyone can add a card to the To Do list at any time.

- Management can change any card in To Do.

- Only management can rearrange a card's priority in the To Do list in relation to another card.

- Only developers can provide or change a card's estimate, and only if that card is still in the To Do list.

- Once a card is scheduled, it cannot be modified, except by adding comments and checklists.

- Management may not touch cards that are in Current Iteration or Doing lists. They may comment on them freely, however.

- Developers assign themselves to cards during daily planning meetings. Management should never dictate who implements which cards.

- A developer can only be assigned to one card in the Doing list at a time.

- Only one developer should be assigned to a card. If multiple developers are assigned, it is a sign that the card is too complex and should be broken up.

- If a developer does not complete a card, it can be put back in the Current Iteration list to be finished later.

Resources

- Trello [raw URL: www.trello.com/]

- Scrum for Trello [raw URL: https://scrumfortrello.com/]

Feedback

If you use Agile to manage your software development, and have other ideas and suggestions that help make your team more effective, I'd love to hear about them.

CHAPTER 26

Pixabay.com Image Repository

Where to get Creative Commons licensed images for almost any purpose? One day I was looking for a picture of a swimming pool for a mobile app I was writing. Much to my excitement, I stumbled upon an online image catalog called Pixabay (`https://pixabay.com`).

Overview

Pixabay claims to have over 4,100,000 images that can be used free of charge. Their terms of service indicate that every image is bound to the CC0 Public Domain license, which puts them into the public domain, and thus can be used for any legal purpose.

As of August 2023, Pixabay offers a variety of media types:

- Images: photos, vector graphics, animated GIFs, and illustrations

- Videos

- Music

In this chapter, I focus on images, but videos and music work the same way.

© Michael D. Callaghan 2024
M. D. Callaghan, *Angular for Business*, https://doi.org/10.1007/978-1-4842-9609-7_26

Image Search

The site is attractive and easy to use. I typed "swimming pool" into the search box and was quickly rewarded with more than 2300 images to review.

When searching for an image, you can choose a single image type or all. I changed my search to include only photos, which reduced my search results to just over 2100. Obviously most of their images of swimming pools are photographs.

There are more search options available. You can search by portrait or landscape orientation, which Pixabay calls vertical or horizontal. You can also search by category, dominant color, transparent, or even black and white images. The end result is that it is easy to find the right image for your needs.

The search results are conveniently organized into a grid resembling a light box that most people will find intuitive. The first row of images is "sponsored" by iStock. I get it. That is how they make their money. Quite frankly, the free images are of no lesser quality than the sponsored ones.

Navigating the search results is simple. There are pager controls at the top and bottom of the grid. It irritates me whenever I see a website that only has pager controls at the top or bottom. How hard is it to do both? Further demonstrating their understanding of how most people will browse the search results, there is a big "Next page" button at the bottom. As you hover over an image, you can see its tags along with the number of people who have "liked" or "favorited" the image.

Some images may be identified as "Adult Content." You cannot see the image until you click on it and accept the warning. You can turn this feature off, but I tend to leave it on. Though there are some nudes on the site, I have yet to see anything I would consider pornographic. Their opinion of what constitutes adult content errs on the side of caution. That said, you have been warned.

Image Details

Clicking on an image takes you to its detail page, containing the artist name, how long ago the image was uploaded, how many times it has been viewed and downloaded, and its license. So far, I have only seen licenses that are "Free for commercial use/No attribution required." Some images include the details of the camera that took the pictures and its settings (shutter speed, lens focal length, aperture, etc.). Below the image are thumbnails of similar images from the site. There is also a small collection of iStock-sponsored images that I found to be somewhat related to the image selected.

At one time, Pixabay required you to register if you wanted to download any of their images. That seemed fair, but appears no longer to be the case. I have been a registered user for about eight years now. Registration is free and quick. They do not even require any personal information other than your email address. In the years since I signed up, they have never sent me a single email or bothered me in any way. Nor have I suddenly and mysteriously been inundated with ads for the types of images I have searched for.

Registered or not, you can download an image from its detail page. Simply select the image size you want. There are usually four options. Then click the big green Download button. The actual image dimensions and file sizes are conveniently displayed, so you will be sure you get the exact image you want.

Thank the Artist

Pixabay appears to be trying to make itself a social network of media, and it has all of the tools you'd expect to make that happen. You can "like" images, leave comments, mark an image as a favorite, or share it on

Facebook and Instagram. You can even follow or message a favorite artist. Intelligent hyperlinks throughout the site let you immediately find other images by the same artist, taken by the same camera, etc.

One of my favorite features is the Donate button. On an image detail page is a green button labeled "Donate." When you download an image, you are presented again with a similar button. Clicking it will take you to PayPal.com, where you can contribute any amount you feel appropriate to the artist. I presume many of their artists use Pixabay as a portfolio, and as a way to get noticed.

Pixabay for Artists

If you are a fledgling artist, or even a seasoned professional, Pixabay makes it easy for you to upload your own photos. They have a full page describing their image quality guidelines, along with plenty of examples of what not to submit. There is even a list of image tags their users are searching for. If you upload ten or more photos, they say they will remove all ads. I haven't tried this yet, but I might.

If you have your own portfolio of images, Pixabay is a great way to set up an online portfolio.

Summary

In summary, Pixabay contains an impressive collection of high-quality, beautiful and useful images, all free of charge, that can be used for practically any purpose you can imagine. Not only did I find the perfect background image I needed, I found an image to use as a splash screen, and even a mobile application icon. The process was quick and simple. And it sure beats paying tens or even hundreds of dollars for a "professional" image.

Index

A

© Michael D. Callaghan 2024
M. D. Callaghan, *Angular for Business*, https://doi.org/10.1007/978-1-4842-9609-7

C

W, X, Y, Z

Printed in the United States
by Baker & Taylor Publisher Services